Cognitive differentiation: a structural variable underlying the Fishbein attitude model

Richard Miller Durand, Martin Fishbein

Nabu Public Domain Reprints:

You are holding a reproduction of an original work published before 1923 that is in the public domain in the United States of America, and possibly other countries. You may freely copy and distribute this work as no entity (individual or corporate) has a copyright on the body of the work. This book may contain prior copyright references, and library stamps (as most of these works were scanned from library copies). These have been scanned and retained as part of the historical artifact.

This book may have occasional imperfections such as missing or blurred pages, poor pictures, errant marks, etc. that were either part of the original artifact, or were introduced by the scanning process. We believe this work is culturally important, and despite the imperfections, have elected to bring it back into print as part of our continuing commitment to the preservation of printed works worldwide. We appreciate your understanding of the imperfections in the preservation process, and hope you enjoy this valuable book.

ACKNOWLEDGMENTS

Sincere appreciation is offered to members of the supervisory committee: Dr. Zarrel V. Lambert, Dr. R. Eugene Klippel, Dr. Ralph B. Thompson, Dr. Jack Feldman, and Dr. Robert C. Ziller. The author would especially like to express his debt of gratitude to Dr. Zarrel V. Lambert, chairman of the supervisory committee. The two years spent as his graduate assistant was a very worthwhile learning experience.

In addition, the author would like to express his appreciation to Dr. Donald B. Butterworth for introducing him to the study of Marketing, Dr. Franz R. Epting for introducing him to the field of cognition, and to Dr. Olli T. Ahtola for his unselfish hours of instruction on attitude theory.

TABLE OF CONTENTS

	Page
ACKNOWLEDGMENTS	iii
LIST OF TABLES	vii
LIST OF FIGURES	x
ABSTRACT	xi

CHAPTER

I   INTRODUCTION 1

    Problem Definition 1
    Concepts of Attitude and Cognitive
      Complexity 3
      Concept of Attitude 3
      Concept of Cognitive Complexity . . 5

II   CONCEPTUAL FRAMEWORK 10

    Attitude Measurement Through Expectancy-
      Value Models 10
      Rosenberg 11
      Adequacy-Importance 13
      Issues Related to the Adequacy-
        Importance Model 14
      Fishbein Model 20
    Cognitive Differentiation: Measurement
      and Meaning 27
      Approaches by Scott and Crockett . 27
      Bieri's Theory and Measurement . . 28
      Generalizability of Cognitive
        Differentiation Across Content
        Domains 35

III   RESEARCH HYPOTHESES 40

    Hypothesis 1 41
    Hypothesis 2 42
    Hypothesis 3 42
    Marketing Implications 43

TABLE OF CONTENTS (continued)

CHAPTER		Page
IV	METHODOLOGY.	46
	Research Design	46
	Product Selection.	46
	Sample Selection	47
	Instrument Design.	48
	Instrument Pretest	57
	Hypothesis Operationalization and Analysis.	57
	Hypothesis 1: Cognitive Differentiation and the Number of Cognitive Elements.	58
	Hypothesis 2: Predictive Efficacy of the Intra-Individual versus Cross-Sectional Analytic Procedures in the Attitude Model.	68
	Hypothesis 3: Generalizability of Cognitive Differentiation.	71
V	RESULTS AND DISCUSSION	72
	Hypothesis 1: Cognitive Differentiation and the Number of Cognitive Elements.	72
	Toothpaste	72
	Automobiles.	75
	Hypothesis 2: Predictive Efficacy of the Intra-Individual versus Cross-Sectional Analytic Procedures in the Attitude Model	77
	Toothpaste	78
	Automobiles.	80
	Hypothesis 3: Generalizability of Cognitive Differentiation.	88
	Aberrations of the Fishbein Attitude Model: The Effects of Their Deletion on Study Results.	90
	Hypothesis 1: Cognitive Differentiation and the Number of Cognitive Elements	91
	Hypothesis 2: Predictive Efficacy of the Intra-Individual versus Cross-Sectional Analytic Procedures in the Attitude Model.	95

TABLE OF CONTENTS (continued)

CHAPTER		Page
VI	CONCLUSION	112
	Hypothesis 1: Cognitive Differentiation and the Number of Cognitive Elements.	112
	Hypothesis 2. Predictive Efficacy of the Intra-Individual versus Cross-Sectional Analytic Procedures in the Attitude Model.	114
	Hypothesis 3: Generalizability of Cognitive Differentiation	117
	Areas for Further Research.	117

APPENDICES

I-A	TOOTHPASTE INSTRUMENT.	121
I-B	AUTOMOBILES INSTRUMENT	133
I-C	INTERPERSONAL GRID INSTRUMENT.	148
I-D	QUESTIONNAIRE (Toothpaste)	152
I-E	QUESTIONNAIRE (Automobiles).	155
II	FREQUENCY DISTRIBUTION OF CORRELATION COEFFICIENTS	158

REFERENCES. 163

BIOGRAPHICAL SKETCH 175

LIST OF TABLES

TABLE		Page
1	BIERI'S MODIFICATION OF THE REPTEST FOR ASSESSING COGNITIVE DIFFERENTIATION	30
2	ATTRIBUTES ELICITED FOR TOOTHPASTE	49
3	ATTRIBUTES ELICITED FOR AUTOMOBILES	50
4	CORRELATIONS BETWEEN NUMBER OF COGNITIVE ELEMENTS AND COGNITIVE DIFFERENTIATION SCORE FOR TOOTHPASTE	73
5	CORRELATIONS BETWEEN NUMBER OF COGNITIVE ELEMENTS AND COGNITIVE DIFFERENTIATION SCORE FOR AUTOMOBILES	76
6	CORRELATION COEFFICIENTS DERIVED FROM INTRA-INDIVIDUAL AND CROSS-SECTIONAL ANALYSES FOR TOOTHPASTE	79
7	CORRELATION COEFFICIENTS DERIVED FROM INTRA-INDIVIDUAL AND CROSS-SECTIONAL ANALYSES FOR AUTOMOBILES	81
8	CORRELATION COEFFICIENTS BASED ON STANDARDIZED AND NON-STANDARDIZED DATA FOR DIFFERENT ENTRANCE PROCEDURES--CROSS-SECTIONAL ANALYSIS	85
9	CORRELATION MATRIX BETWEEN DIFFERENTIATION LEVELS FOR THREE COGNITIVE DOMAINS	89
10	CORRELATIONS BETWEEN NUMBER OF COGNITIVE ELEMENTS AND COGNITIVE DIFFERENTIATION BY ENTRANCE METHOD FOR TOOTHPASTE AND AUTOMOBILES --ELEMENTS ENTERED IN THE SAME ORDER	92
11	CORRELATIONS BETWEEN NUMBER OF COGNITIVE ELEMENTS AND COGNITIVE DIFFERENTIATION BY ENTRANCE METHOD FOR TOOTHPASTE AND AUTOMOBILES --ELEMENT ORDER ALLOWED TO VARY	93

LIST OF TABLES (continued)

TABLE		Page
12	MEAN CORRELATION COEFFICIENTS DERIVED FROM THE INTRA-INDIVIDUAL ANALYSIS FOR TOOTHPASTE--COGNITIVE ELEMENTS ENTERED IN THE SAME ORDER.	96
13	MEAN CORRELATION COEFFICIENTS DERIVED FROM THE INTRA-INDIVIDUAL ANALYSIS FOR TOOTHPASTE--COGNITIVE ELEMENT ENTRANCE ORDER PERMITTED TO VARY	97
14	MEAN CORRELATION COEFFICIENTS DERIVED FROM THE INTRA-INDIVIDUAL ANALYSIS FOR AUTOMOBILES--COGNITIVE ELEMENTS ENTERED IN THE SAME ORDER	98
15	MEAN CORRELATION COEFFICIENTS DERIVED FROM THE INTRA-INDIVIDUAL ANALYSIS FOR AUTOMOBILES--COGNITIVE ELEMENT ENTRANCE ORDER PERMITTED TO VARY	99
16	MEAN COGNITIVE DIFFERENTIATION SCORES FOR AUTOMOBILES--COGNITIVE ELEMENT ENTRANCE ORDER PERMITTED TO VARY	102
17	MEAN COGNITIVE DIFFERENTIATION SCORES FOR AUTOMOBILES--COGNITIVE ELEMENTS ENTERED IN SAME ORDER	103
18	MEAN COGNITIVE DIFFERENTIATION SCORES FOR TOOTHPASTE--COGNITIVE ELEMENT ENTRANCE ORDER PERMITTED TO VARY	104
19	MEAN COGNITIVE DIFFERENTIATION SCORES FOR TOOTHPASTE--COGNITIVE ELEMENTS ENTERED IN THE SAME ORDER.	105
20	MEAN NUMBER OF COGNITIVE ELEMENTS FOR AUTOMOBILES--COGNITIVE ELEMENT ENTRANCE ORDER PERMITTED TO VARY	107
21	MEAN NUMBER OF COGNITIVE ELEMENTS FOR AUTOMOBILES--COGNITIVE ELEMENTS ENTERED IN SAME ORDER.	108

LIST OF TABLES (continued)

TABLE		Page
22	MEAN NUMBER OF COGNITIVE ELEMENTS FOR TOOTHPASTE--COGNITIVE ELEMENTS ENTRANCE ORDER PERMITTED TO VARY	109
23	MEAN NUMBER OF COGNITIVE ELEMENTS FOR DIFFERENT ENTRANCE PROCEDURES AND COGNITIVE DIFFERENTIATION SCORE FOR TOOTHPASTE--COGNITIVE ELEMENTS ENTERED IN THE SAME ORDER.	110

LIST OF FIGURES

FIGURE		Page
1	STAGED ENTRANCE PROCEDURE	60
2	PLOT OF CORRELATION COEFFICIENTS BETWEEN THE PREDICTED AND ELICITED ATTITUDE AS THE NUMBER OF COGNITIVE ELEMENTS VARIES	63

Abstract of Dissertation Presented to the Graduate Council
of the University of Florida in Partial Fulfillment
of the Requirements for the Degree of Doctor of Philosophy

COGNITIVE DIFFERENTIATION: A STRUCTURAL VARIABLE
UNDERLYING THE FISHBEIN ATTITUDE MODEL

By

Richard M. Durand

August, 1975

Chairman: Zarrel V. Lambert
Major Department: Marketing

Recent emphasis of consumer behavior research has dealt with the use of various expectancy-value attitude models in an attempt to gain a better understanding of consumers' perceptions of products and hence their purchasing behavior. These attitude models attempt to predict attitude from the system of beliefs an individual holds about a product or brand.

Much of the current work on the prediction of attitudes, however, fails to take into consideration individual differences in the structure of cognition. In operationalizing the attitude models, the implicit assumption is that cognitive structure, composed of the interrelationship and organization of beliefs, is the same for each individual. This is reflected in the use of attitude instruments with a standard set of belief statements to predict attitude. The concept of cognitive differentiation (a structural variable of cognition), on the other hand, points out that attitudes concerning a range of stimuli in a product category can be based on few or many units of information and that this range varies from individual to individual.

The purpose of this study was to investigate the effect of cognitive differentiation on the predictive efficacy of an expectancy-value model of attitudes, more specifically the Fishbein model.

Bieri's Reptest was used to measure cognitive differentiation. The product categories investigated in this study were automobiles and toothpaste. One hundred two male students from Southern Illinois University at Carbondale participated in the study.

Three hypotheses were presented and analyzed in the study. The first hypothesis was that the optimal number of cognitive elements, in terms of predictive efficacy, for the Fishbein model, was positively related to cognitive differentiation. Six different entrance procedures were used to enter the cognitive elements into the Fishbein attitude model. Each of the entrance procedures was applied in two ways: (1) the cognitive element order was permitted to vary and (2) all elements were entered in the same order across all respondents.

No significant correlation coefficients between the optimal number of cognitive elements and differentiation were found in the case for automobiles. The largest correlation for toothpaste was .31. Although significant it was not large enough to warrant the rejection of the null hypothesis. It is interesting to note, however, that all of the relationships for automobiles and toothpaste were in the predicted direction, except in one instance.

The second hypothesis dealt with comparing the predictive efficacy of the intra-individual versus cross-sectional analytic procedures in applying the Fishbein attitude model. The results indicated that the predictive efficiency of the attitude model is greater when the analytic procedure is based on an intra-individual analysis rather than a cross-sectional one.

Three cognitive domains were included in examining the third hypothesis that cognitive differentiation was generalizable across different domains. These domains were automobiles, toothpaste, and interpersonal relations. The intercorrelations between the differentiation scores for each domain, although significant, were too low for the construct of cognitive differentiation to be considered generalizable.

CHAPTER I

INTRODUCTION

Problem Definition

Recent emphasis of consumer behavior research has dealt with the use of various attitude models in an attempt to gain a better understanding of consumers' perception of products and to predict and gain insight into the behavior of consumers. These attitude models attempt to predict attitude from an individual's system of beliefs or perceptions held about a product or brand. With a better understanding of the beliefs underlying an attitude, marketing strategies can be developed in a more efficient manner and demands by consumers more effectively met

Much of the current work on the prediction of attitudes, however, fails to take into consideration individual differences in the structure of cognition. In operationalizing the attitude models the implicit assumption is that the cognitive structure, composed of the interrelationship and organization of beliefs, is the same for each individual. This is reflected in the use of attitude instruments with a standard set of belief statements used to predict attitude.

The purpose of this study, therefore, is to investigate the effect of a structural variable of cognition (cognitive differentiation) on the predictive efficacy of an attitude model. If the predictive efficacy is increased by taking into account individual differences in cognitive structure, then the usefulness of the attitude model will be improved with greater insight into the underlying beliefs of an attitude.

The attitude model which will be examined is the one postulated by Fishbein [29, 30, 31, 32] and the structural variable will be cognitive differentiation postulated by Bieri [12, 13, 15, 17]. In Fishbein's model, an attitude is considered to be a function of the strength of an individual's beliefs about an attitude object and the evaluation of those beliefs. Cognitive differentiation, on the other hand, refers fundamentally to the extent to which an individual distinguishes between a set of objects. In a marketing context, an individual with a differentiated cognitive system has the capacity to view attitude objects in a multidimensional way because more dimensions (beliefs) are available for product perception. An individual with a relatively undifferentiated system can be expected to hold beliefs that are relatively homogeneous or similar to one another, thereby limiting product perception to fewer dimensions.

Concepts of Attitude and Cognitive Complexity

The purpose of this study is to investigate the relationship between an expectancy-value attitude model and cognitive differentiation (a cognitive complexity variable). In light of this goal, this section is developed to present the broad theoretical framework on which this study is based. More specifically, the concept of attitude will be defined and the two major schools of thought dealing with the composition of attitudes will be discussed. Furthermore, the concept of cognitive complexity will be defined and a theoretical tie between the two concepts will be established.

Concept of Attitude

There are virtually as many definitions of attitudes as there are major attitude theorists. One definition of attitude on which most researchers seem to agree is one proposed by Gordon Allport. He defined attitude as "a mental and neural state of readiness, organized through experience, exerting a directive or dynamic influence upon the individual's response to all objects and situations with which it is related" [4, p. 45].

This definition leaves a good deal of room for different interpretations as to the theoretical conception of the composition of an attitude. There are two major schools on the issue of the composition of an attitude. One school, currently headed by Fishbein [30, 31, 32] and supported by Shaw and Wright [74] and Thurstone [81], treats attitude as a unidimensional concept. The second school conceptualizes attitude in a multidimentional manner. Advocates of this position include, among others, Krech, Crutchfield, and Ballachey [60], Katz and Stotland [41], and Rosenberg and Hovland [63].

Fishbein, following Thurstone [81], treats attitude as a unidimensional concept of affect. This affective component encompasses the evaluation, feelings of like or dislike, of an attitude object by an individual. The cognitive component, which refers primarily to how the attitude object is perceived (beliefs about the object), is viewed as being related to attitudes by Fishbein [32, pp. 478-9]. These beliefs held by an individual toward an object are determinants of attitude and not a part of the attitude [32, p. 479].

The group of theorists who view attitude as a multidimensional concept conceive attitude as containing conative (behavioral) and cognitive components in addition to the affective component. While this theoretical approach to attitude has a number of supporters, surprisingly few attempts have been made at operationalizing this multidimensional approach to attitudes [e.g., 49].

Several major reasons have been proposed for treating attitude as unidimensional concept of affect rather than as a three-component concept. First, in most cases only the affective component is measured by attitude researchers even if they are proponents of the tripartite conceptualization of attitude [32, p. 479]. Second, treating attitude as a unidimensional concept of affect is on a firmer theoretical base and describes the true state of affairs more adequately [74, p. 11]. Third, the operationalization of a multidimensional view of attitude is far more difficult than using a unidimensional affect measure. Finally, the single affect score has been shown to be highly related to an individual's beliefs about the object by Zajonc [93], Fishbein [31], and Rosenberg [60, 61].

Concept of Cognitive Complexity

Whether attitude is treated as a unidimensional measure of affect or is viewed as a multidimensional concept, the cognitive component plays an important role. In the former case, this component is used in the prediction of affect (attitude) while in the latter it is one of the three parts of an attitude. Both conceptualizations basically treat the cognitive component as being comprised of the various beliefs that an individual holds about a given attitude object [32, 41, 50]. The concern then, in an attitudinal framework, is the identification and subsequent measurement of the magnitude and direction of these beliefs (or elements of cognition).

The present study is delving beyond the examination of the cognitive component in terms of content (magnitude and direction of beliefs) and will be investigating the interrelationship and organization of the beliefs. This interrelationship and organization of the elements in the cognitive component refers to an individual's cognitive structure [17, p. 185; 71, p. 405; 92, p. 321; 93, p. 159]. These cognitive structures have been hypothesized to play a significant role in a number of psychological properties such as perception, learning, and other psychological processes [74, p. 173]. Therefore, it is postulated that cognitive structures also play a role in attitude formation.

In order to describe the organization and relationship between the cognitive elements, a number of morphological properties of cognitive structures have been proposed. These properties have generally been grouped under the broad heading "cognitive complexity" [79]. Cognitive complexity, while there is no single body of theory that entirely encompasses the concept, is generally considered to be associated with an underlying response rather than with what an individual perceives. In other words, complexity is concerned with the number of cognitive elements used and the organization of them in cognitive space. The greater the cognitive complexity of an individual the more versatile a system he will have for perceiving objects, events, or people due to the relationship and organization of the cognitive elements.

The two most accepted approaches to the study of complexity, although a number have been proposed [e.g., 69, 93], are cognitive differentiation and cognitive integration. Differentiation refers to the relative number of dimensions used by an individual and, more specifically, reflects the extent to which an individual's system of constructs or cognitive dimensions can distinguish between a set of objects in a cognitive domain. In other words, a differentiated individual will utilize a greater number of dimensions in interpreting and perceiving an object than will a less differentiated individual. In an attitudinal framework, the differentiated individual may hold more beliefs about an attitude object than will one who is less differentiated. Cognitive integration, on the other hand, is defined as "the extent to which dimensional units of information can be interrelated in different ways in order to generate new and discrepant perspectives about stimuli" [65, p 25]. An individual who is cognitively integrated can combine various independent dimensions concerning an object, thereby enabling alternative interpretations or perceptions of the object.

Both of these approaches, differentiation and integration, appear to be reasonably close in that differentiation seems to be a precondition for integration [78, p. 154]. Several authors have attempted to explain the relationship between these two concepts on a theoretical level. Witkin et al. [89] theorized that in order to have greater differentiation a more complex reintegration of the system was necessary. Harvey, Hunt, and Schroder, who are primarily integration theorists, state that "differentiation does not necessitate integration," but rather "integration must be preceded by differentiation" [36, p. 22]. Schroder, Driver, and Streufert, while arguing that differentiation is not a key aspect of integration, state that with greater differentiation there is a higher probability of integrative complexity [65, p. 166].

In an attempt to ascertain whether integration and differentiation are disparate processes, a number of empirical studies have been carried out using various techniques for measuring these variables. Wyer [91] found that his model of integration was unrelated to either his conceptualization of differentiation or that of Scott [71]. Vannoy [85] found that integration, as measured by Schroder and Streuferts' Sentence Complextion Test [66], was not significantly correlated with Bieri's measure of differentiation [17]. Findings by Streufert and Fromkin [78] have also been reported as showing little or no correlation between various measures of differentiation and integration. Since there is no apparent empirical support for treating integration and differentiation as related processes, a decision must be made on which one to utilize in examining how a structural variable of cognition relates to an attitude model.

This study will focus on cognitive differentiation rather than integration for several reasons. First, the concept of differentiation has been espoused by several authors as being useful in a number of different domains of interest [e.g., 7, 27, 73]. In other words, the theory and instruments designed to measure differentiation can be readily modified to be applicable for a number of different cognitive domains. Differentiation instruments can be developed for product and/or brand categories, thereby making it possible to implement this concept in the study of consumer behavior. Second, differentiation has a strong theoretical base from which predictions can be made and implications drawn. Third, differentiation has received a greater amount of attention in the psychological literature and is conceptually clearer than integration. Finally, being perhaps one of the simpler properties of a cognitive structure [27, p. 6], it is an appropriate place to begin the conceptualization of the tie between attitudes and cognitive structure. The exclusion of integration from this study does by no means imply that integration is not applicable to attitude research. Rather, it is felt that its introduction into attitude research might be more appropriate after exploratory research is conducted into the relevance of differentiation.

CHAPTER II

CONCEPTUAL FRAMEWORK

Attitude Measurement Through Expectancy-Value Models

The measurement of attitudes through expectancy-value attitude models has gained wide support in marketing as evidenced by the increasing number of published articles in the area. The reasons for this support are numerous. Through the use of this approach to attitude measurement, for example, it is possible to obtain a greater amount of information pertaining to the cognitive elements underlying an attitude toward an object than if more traditional measures are used (e.g., Likert and Thurstone scales) [1, p. 13]. The increased information is useful in providing a greater understanding of consumers' perceptions of the strengths and weaknesses of products on relevant attributes. This facilitates the development and improvement of marketing strategies.

In light of the advantages that the expectancy-value orientation to attitudes has over other more traditional approaches, there are three major goals to this section. First, the Rosenberg [60, 61, 62], adequacy-importance, and Fishbein [29, 30, 31, 32, 33] models will be presented. While other expectancy-value attitude models exist [e.g., 1, 58, 93], these are the three basic underlying models. Second, the empirical results of a number of studies will be provided to illustrate the applicability of these attitude formulations to various product categories in marketing. Finally, a number of studies reporting various modifications of these models will be examined. The primary purpose of this is to present a number of issues dealing with improving the predictive validity of attitude models. These issues will be presented primarily in the adequacy-importance model section

Rosenberg

In order to examine the structural relationships between attitudes and beliefs about the attitude object, Rosenberg [61] utilizes an instrumentality-value or means-end approach. This type of analysis assumes that "an attitude toward any object or situation is related to the ends which the object serves; i.e., to its consequences" [57, p. 153]. To investigate the relationship between attitude and an individual's cognitive structure (beliefs about the attitude object), Rosenberg hypothesized that [61, p. 367]:

> The degree and sign of affect aroused in an individual by an object (as reflected by the position he chooses on an attitude scale) vary as a function of the algebraic sum of the products obtained by multiplying the rated importance of each value

associated with that object by the rated potency of the object for achieving or blocking the realization of that value.

Algebraically, this hypothesis has been expressed in model form as [29, p. 394]:

$$A_o = \sum_{i=1}^{n} I_i V_i ;$$

where

A_o = the attitude toward the object o,

I_i = the belief or probability that the object will lead to or block the attainment of a given valued state "i",

V_i = the "value importance" or amount of affect expected from the valued state "i", and

n = the number of beliefs.

This hypothesis was confirmed by Rosenberg through the use of a chi-square procedure.

While the Rosenberg model has not been employed extensively in predicting attitude in a marketing framework, various studies have utilized this model. Bither and Miller [18] used the Rosenberg model to investigate its applicability as an index to differentiate among univariate affect ratings of various types of automobiles. The index was derived from the predicted attitude portion ($\sum_{i=1}^{n} I_i V_i$) of the model. They found that the subject's position on a univariate rating of brand appeal (affect) was highly associated with the value importance and attitude object instrumentality index. This finding was supported whether a cross-sectional (inter-subject) analysis or intra-individual analysis procedure was employed.

Hansen [35] and Klippel and Bither [48] concentrated their analysis among lower-priced items. The applicability of the Rosenberg model in the prediction of choices among menu items, hairdryers, restaurants, and books was shown by Hansen. His findings also indicated that both components of the Rosenberg model (I and V) added significantly to the predictive value of the overall attractiveness score (affect) Klippel and Bither found the model to be predictive of consumers' choices between brands of mouthwash although the correlations were low.

Adequacy-Importance[1]

The adequacy-importance model is the most widely used attitude model in research on consumer behavior. It is a variation of the Rosenberg model [59, 60, 62] and the Fishbein model [29, 30, 31] which is discussed in the next section. Two primary arguments for deviating from the "pure" Fishbein-Rosenberg formulations have been presented. One suggests that the different methods of analysis are due to "differences in purpose between attitude theories developed in social psychology and brand preference" [8,

---

[1] The name "adequacy-importance" was used by Cohen, Fishbein, and Ahtola [23] in their rebuttal to the Sheth-Talarzyk [76] and Bass-Talarzyk [10] and by Ahtola [1].

p. 461]. The second argument is based on alternative interpretations to a given theory [75]. The basic adequacy-importance model can be expressed quantitatively as [1, p. 35]:

$$A_o = \sum_{i=1}^{n} P_i D_i;$$

where

A_o = an individual's attitude toward o,

P_i = importance of attribute (dimension) i for the person,

D_i = his evaluation of o with respect to the attribute dimension i, and

n = number of attribute dimensions.

This model has been used by Bass and Talarzyk [10], Sheth and Talarzyk [76], Wilkie and McCann [86], Hansen [35], Bass, Pessemier, and Lehmann [9], Wilkie and Weinreich [88], Moinpour and MacLachlan [54], and Scott and Bennett [67], among others.

Issues Related to the Adequacy-Importance Model

The purpose of this section is to focus primarily on several issues centering around increasing the predictive validity of the adequacy-importance attitude model.[2] The issues of major concern in this analysis include (1) the

---

[2] An extensive review of the research on expectancy-value models in marketing and the issues associated with the predictability of the models is discussed in detail by Wilkie and Pessemier [87].

use of an intra-individual (within-individual) or cross-sectional (inter-individual) analytic procedure, (2) the normalization of the individual components of the model, and (3) the number of cognitive elements ($P_i D_i$) used and the order in which the elements are entered into the predictive portion of the equation ($\Sigma P_i D_i$).

The results of two studies based on a common data bank with essentially the same attitude model formulation illustrate the issue of using an intra-individual versus cross-sectional analytic procedure. Sheth and Talarzyk used a simple regression procedure in examining the relationship between a preference scale (attitude) for a given brand and the predicted attitude derived from the adequacy-importance model shown above. Analysis was on a cross-sectional basis with the resultant average r^2s ranging from .013 to .057 when both components of the model (P_i and D_i) were used. When only the belief component was included, the average r^2s for each product category examined ranged from .091 to .179. This is well below many other studies using different statistical procedures.

In the study performed by Bass and Talarzyk, the analysis was conducted at the individual, rather than cross-sectional level using confusion matrices. Their results, although not directly comparable to the Sheth and Talarzyk findings, provided strong evidence that the model was, in fact, useful to explain brand preference. Examples of other studies where the analysis was on an intra-individual basis includes studies by Nakanishi and Bettman [56], Wilkie and McCann [86], Hansen [35], Bass, Pessemier, and Lehmann [9], and Wilkie and Weinreich [88] A basic reason for using an intra-individual approach rather than a cross-sectional one is that the latter assumes respondent homogeneity in scale measurement as well as the functional relationship of brand preference to attitudes [87]. In other words, different individuals have different anchor points and response sets which would tend to confound the results if a cross-sectional analysis is employed.

In order to offset this criticism of cross-sectional analysis, Bass and Wilkie [11] have proposed that the components of the model (P_1 and D_1) can be normalized on an intra-individual level. Normalizing these components adjusts the within-subject variance in responses which eliminates the problem of different anchor points and response sets.

Bass and Wilkie, in testing the effect of normalizing the attitude model, utilized the same data base employed by Bass and Talarzyk and Sheth and Talarzyk. The hypothesis, concerning the effects of normalization on the predictive efficacy of the attitude model, was tested by comparing the amount of variance explained between the predicted attitude and brand preference for the non-normalized and normalized responses The average variation explained for the normalized attitude model was .39 compared to .15 for the non-normalized one. This difference is significant at the .001 level.

The final issue to be examined deals with the number of attributes or belief components included in an attitude model to estimate brand preference or attitude. Most authors appear to assume that five to seven attributes are salient (relevant) to the individual and therefore use that many in the attitude model [e.g., 7, 11, 76, 86]. Two studies, those by Churchill [21] and Wilkie and Weinreich [88], have examined the question of how many attributes should be included in the model to predict attitude.[3] Churchill used a cross-sectional procedure whereas Wilkie and Weinreich analyzed their data on an intra-individual basis.

Churchill used a range of attributes rather than using a fixed number of attributes, to examine whether one could increase the predictive validity of the adequacy-importance model[4] by varying the number of attributes included in the model. Each individual was asked to rate two writing pens on 19 product attributes, the importance of each attribute,

---

[3] Nakanishi and Bettman [56] take into consideration the fact that different respondents use different numbers of cognitive elements in their analysis but the manner in which their results are presented prevents any generalization to be made.

[4] Churchill, while claiming to be using the Fishbein model, was in fact using a modification of the adequacy-importance measure

and evaluate each pen. These data yielded 19 preference predictions for each individual based on the order of importance of each attribute for each subject. The first prediction, for example, was based on the attribute considered most important by the individual, the second prediction included the two most important attributes for the individual, and so on. This was done for each subject with each resultant prediction correlated with the actual evaluation of the pens. In other words, 19 correlation coefficients were obtained for the sample, in a cross-sectional manner, with the predicted preference for each subject being composed of different attributes based on their ratings of importance. Churchill found that the predictive accuracy increased, leveled off, and then declined as the number of attributes increased. The correlations between actual and predicted preference ranged from .118 for one attribute, to a peak of .558 for 17 attributes and .552 for 19 attributes.

Wilkie and Weinreich [88] asked a sample of 29 housewives to rate seven supermarkets on seven store attributes. Four studies were performed so that the various analytic procedures could be compared.[5] The first study followed the more traditional approach to attitude studies in

---

[5]While two attitude models were presented, one with raw scores and the other with normalized scores, only the former will be presented. On an intra-individual design, there is no reason for normalizing the responses.

marketing. All seven attributes were used in predicting preference of stores with the resultant correlation coefficient derived from correlating the predicted and stated preference. The second study allowed the number of attributes, included in the model, to vary from one to seven. A mean determinism score was used to decide the order or attribute entry for the sample. This determinism score[6] incorporates both the importance score for each attribute and the variance in perceived satisfaction on the attributes over all stores. The greater the determinism score the higher the entry of the variable into the model. The third study derived attitude scores based on attributes introduced in the model on an individual basis. In other words, the determinism score for each individual specified the order of attribute entry. The same number of attributes were used for each subject. Finally, in the fourth analysis, each individual's determinism score was used to select the attribute to be entered with the attributes being entered until the maximum correlation with preference was ascertained

The results of this study by Wilkie and Weinreich appear to provide support for the hypothesis that the predictive accuracy of an attitude model can be improved

---

[6]The determinism procedure is presented in detail in the methodology section.

when the number of attributes and order of attribute entry are varied for each individual. They found in study one that when all seven attributes were used, the Spearman Rho was .6. When the number of attributes were varied across all subjects, a Rho of .63 was highest when five attributes were used. The results of study three showed that the maximum Rho was .62 with three attributes. Finally, the highest mean correlation resulted when the attribute entry and number of attributes entered varied on an intra- or within-individual basis, 76

Fishbein Model

Attitude, although treated as a unidimensional concept of affect, is defined by Fishbein as "a compound in which the elements are beliefs and the effective value of the compound is some function of the affective value of the constituent beliefs" [33, p. 488]. In other words, "an attitude toward any object is a function of (1) the strength of his beliefs about the object and (2) the evaluative aspect of those beliefs" [31, p. 117]. Mathematically, Fishbein's model is expressed as [29, p. 395]:

$$A_o = \sum_{i=1}^{n} B_i a_i;$$

where

A_o = the attitude toward the object o,

B_i = the strength of belief i about o, that is, the "probability" or "improbability" that o is associated with some other concept x_i,

a_1 = the evaluative aspect of B_1, that is, the evaluation of x_1, and

n = the number of beliefs about o, that is, the number of responses in the individual's habit-family-hierarchy.

While other theorists might operationalize the concept of attitude somewhat differently than Fishbein, many such as Shaw and Wright [74], Rosenberg [61, 62], and Peak [57] would also support the rationale of this basic functional relationship.

Fishbein defines "belief about an object" operationally as "the 'probability' or 'improbability' that a particular relationship exists between the object of belief (e.g., an attitude object) and any other object, concept, value, or goal" [29, p. 389]. In other words, a belief refers to the probability that a relationship exists between an attitude object (e.g., Colgate toothpaste) and some other concept, object, value or goal (e.g., whitens). The different types of beliefs have been classified into six basic categories by Fishbein. The classification includes [31, pp. 110-111].

1. Beliefs about the component parts of the object.

2. Beliefs about the characteristics, qualities or attributes of the object.

3. Beliefs about the object's relation with other objects or concepts.

4. Beliefs about whether the object will lead to or block attainment of various goals or "valued states".

5. Beliefs about what should be done with respect to the object.

6. Beliefs about what the object should, or should not, be allowed to do.[7]

All of the beliefs held by an individual concerning a given attitude object are viewed as a belief system or habit-family-hierarchy of responses by Fishbein. Following Hull [37], the higher the location of beliefs in the habit hierarchy, the greater the probability that an individual will perceive an association between the attitude object and another object, concept, value or goal. Furthermore, the higher the belief is in the hierarchy, the stronger and more salient it is in the formation and prediction of an attitude.

Fishbein uses a free association test in order to determine which beliefs are salient to an individual out of the infinite number of possible beliefs held toward an attitude object and the hierarchical position of each belief [29, p. 396]. Individuals are presented with an attitude object and asked to list the characteristics which they feel best describe the object. The characteristics obtained are assumed to be those in an individual's habit-family-hierarchy and the order in which the beliefs are elicited are assumed to represent the approximate belief

---

[7] The first four types of beliefs are considered by Fishbein to fall into what most researchers call an individual's cognitive component or structure. Types five and six are action or behaviorally oriented [31, p. 111]. In any event, the first four types are those most frequently used by marketers.

strength ranking. Their relationship between hierarchical position and belief strength was investigated by Kaplan and Fishbein [40]. They found that for the first six and nine beliefs in the response hierarchy, the correlations between hierarchical position and belief strength were .90 and .72, respectively.

The concept of salient beliefs and their location in the habit-family-hierarchy are major components of Fishbein's attitude theory and his model shown in the formula above. According to Fishbein,

> . . . the only beliefs that serve as determinants of an individual's attitude are those that are present in his habit-family-hierarchy of responses. That is, although all of an individual's beliefs about an object serve as indicants of his attitude toward the object, it is only the individual's salient beliefs, i.e., those in his hierarchy, that serve as determinants of attitude. [29, p. 395]

Theoretically, then, the predictive efficacy of Fishbein's model is at least partially dependent on the saliency of beliefs used to predict attitude. By including only the salient beliefs of an individual the best estimate of attitude will be obtained [29, p. 395].

Support for the proposition that the saliency of the beliefs affects the predictive efficacy of the attitude model has been provided by Rosenberg [61] and Kaplan and Fishbein [40]. Rosenberg found that when an individual's salient beliefs were used to estimate affect there was a stronger relationship between affect and the summative portion of his model ($\sum_{i=1}^{n} I_i V_i$) than when all 35 beliefs provided by the experimenter were utilized. Kaplan and Fishbein also found that when only the salient beliefs of each subject were included in the analysis the estimate of attitude was better than when the total set of beliefs elicited by an individual were used.

From a practical standpoint, Fishbein argues that a standard list of beliefs must be provided to the sample rather than having each subject elicit his own beliefs to use in the attitude model [29]. This requires that some decision must be made on the number of beliefs that can be considered to be salient for an individual and therefore how many beliefs should be included in the attitude instrument. The major concern is to reduce the loss of predictive validity resulting from the inclusion of non-salient beliefs which serve to enter some degree of noise into the model. In other words, the predictive efficacy of the Fishbein model is expected to be greater when the proportion of salient to total beliefs is large

The number of beliefs generally considered to be salient for an individual at any one time is from six to eleven [29, p 395]. Empirical support for this statement is found in studies by Woodworth and Schlosberg [90] on span of attention, information processing by Miller [52], and Kaplan and Fishbein [40]. Based on this evidence, usually a list of five to ten beliefs is used for attitude measurement [1, p 23].

The Fishbein model, while being used quite extensively in the area of social psychology, has not been employed in marketing without substantial modification. This is particularly interesting in that the model provides detailed information regarding the belief component of an attitude and has been shown to correlate around .7, generally with independent measures of affect [2].

One marketing study which attempted to use the Fishbein model was reported by Sampson and Harris [64]. They found correlations between the Fishbein model and elicited attitude ranging from .06 to .26. While these correlation coefficients are very low, they do not accurately reflect the predictive validity of the model for marketing use. Sampson and Harris, due to their use of somewhat different scales, inclusion of non-salient belief statements, and measurement of belief statements in an incorrect manner, nullify any conclusions that can be drawn on the Fishbein model based on their results [1, pp 46-8]. Chapman [20], while not presenting specific research findings, reports on a corporation that has been applying the Fishbein model to commercial surveys where correlations of .6 and above have been found.

Even though the Fishbein model has not been used as extensively in the area of marketing as has the adequacy-importance model, Fishbein's formulation will be used in this study. One major argument for using the Fishbein attitude model over the adequacy-importance model is the strong theoretical background underlying the Fishbein model. The adequacy-importance model is a modification of the Fishbein-Rosenberg formulations and does not have a theoretical base independent of them. Furthermore, ample studies have used the Fishbein model, albeit in the psychological arena, and have attested to its predictive validity. Although the Rosenberg model also has a strong theoretical foundation, it is not being selected because the theory is couched in terms of the attitude object's attainment of positively valued states or blocking of negatively valued states.

This conceptualization of cognitive structure is more difficult to operationalize in a marketing context than is Fishbein's theory. Fishbein accepts any kind of salient belief statement which provides greater latitude in the development of the attitude model and increases the information available about the belief system underlying a given attitude

A final reason for selecting the Fishbein model over the other two rests with the psychological concept of cognitive differentiation, discussed in the next section. Fishbein's conceptualization of salience is theoretically tied to differentiation, in that the level of differentiation is hypothesized to affect the number of salient beliefs an individual holds. Furthermore, with the acceptance of any type of belief statement, the operationalization of the Fishbein model is closer than either of the other models discussed to the conceptualization and operationalization of the concept of differentiation used in this study. This similarity in the operationalization of cognitive differentiation and the Fishbein attitude model will be developed more fully in Chapter IV where the measurement methodology is presented in detail.

Cognitive Differentiation: Measurement and Meaning

The concept of cognitive differentiation is a structural property of cognition. It refers to the degree to which an individual distinguishes among the elements in a given cognitive domain. More specifically, an individual who has a more differentiated cognitive system or structure has the capacity to view or perceive objects, persons, and events in a more multidimensional way than one with a less differentiated system [14, 16].

Approaches by Scott and Crockett

A number of measurement techniques for assessing cognitive differentiation have been proposed. Scott [68, 70, 71], for example, devised a method of measuring differentiation based on information theory [6]. Scott either provides or has subjects generate a list of objects, such as nations, and then asks them to sort the objects into various groups that belong together based on common attributes held by each. From this sorting procedure, a dispersion measure is derived which is interpreted to represent the number of groups-worth of information yielded by the classification system of an individual. The major assumption underlying this differentiation measure is that attributes are dichotomous. In other words, an object is sorted into one category or another based on whether or not it contains a particular attribute. Crockett [24], rather than using a sorting procedure to measure differentiation, developed a technique whereby short essays, written about the stimulus object (people), were analyzed. Cognitive differentiation was defined as "the number of interpersonal constructs in these descriptions . . . " [24, p 51].

Bieri's Theory and Measurement

Bieri, in defining differentiation[8] "as the capacity to construe social behavior in a multidimensional way" [17, p. 185], assumes that differentiation can be measured in terms of the dimensional characteristics of a cognitive structure [15]. This dimensional analysis of cognitive structure has been drawn and modified from George A. Kelly's Personal Construct Theory [44]. Because Bieri's underlying theory and measurement technique is based on Kelly's work,

---

[8] Bieri uses the term cognitive complexity in essentially the same way that most complexity theorists call cognitive differentiation. Therefore, so as to limit any confusion due to differences in terminology, the term differentiation will be used.

part of Kelly's theory and a description of his instrument will be provided

Construct theory, as espoused by Kelly, centers on the fundamental idea that "a person's processes are psychologically channelized by the ways in which man anticipates events" [42, p. 46]. These ways by which events are anticipated and the cognitive world construed are called constructs. In other words, constructs are dimensions or elements used by individuals to characterize how some events, objects, or people are similar but yet different from other events, objects, or people. An example of a construct possibly used by an individual in construing toothpaste is expensive-inexpensive Some brands are viewed as being expensive and others as not. Constructs are assumed to be bipolar in nature.

The Role Construct Reperatory Test (Reptest) was developed by Kelly to provide a means of examining the constructs used by an individual to construe and give structure to his environment. In the "gridform" of the Reptest, a subject is typically presented with a list of 20 to 30 different role figures (e.g., father, mother, girlfriend). These figures are written down at the top of a rectangle, much like that of Table 1 showing Bieri's Technique. The subject is asked to consider, in groups of three, how two of the individuals listed are alike and different from the third in some important aspect.

TABLE 1

BIERI'S MODIFICATION OF THE REPTEST FOR
ASSESSING COGNITIVE DIFFERENTIATION[a]

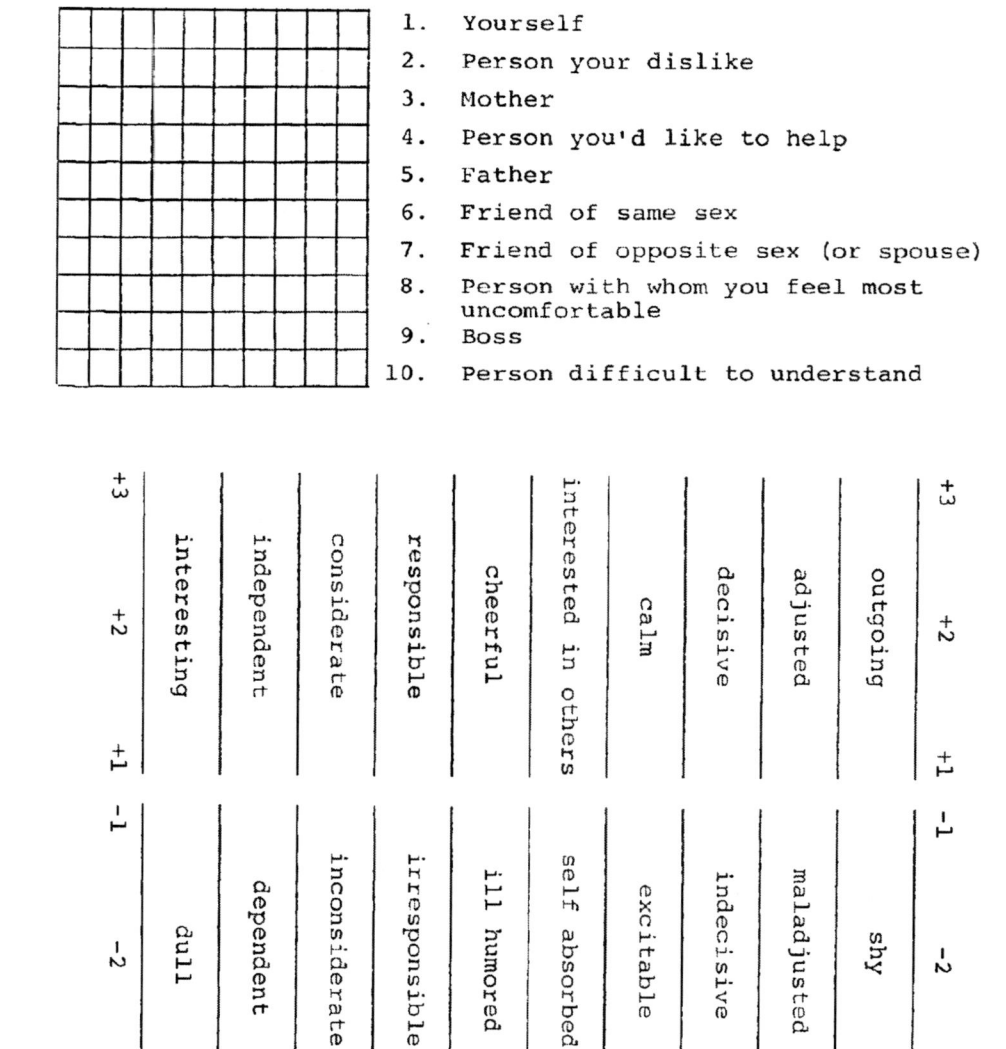

1. Yourself
2. Person your dislike
3. Mother
4. Person you'd like to help
5. Father
6. Friend of same sex
7. Friend of opposite sex (or spouse)
8. Person with whom you feel most uncomfortable
9. Boss
10. Person difficult to understand

+3	+3
+2 interesting	+2 outgoing
+2 independent	+2 adjusted
+2 considerate	+2 decisive
+2 responsible	+2 calm
+2 cheerful	+2 interested in others
+1	+1
-1	-1
-2 dull	-2 shy
-2 dependent	-2 maladjusted
-2 inconsiderate	-2 indecisive
-2 irresponsible	-2 excitable
-2 ill humored	-2 self absorbed
-3	-3

[a]Source: Bieri et al. [17, p. 191].

This construct dimension is written in bipolar form such as pretty-ugly along the right side of the rectangle. Then the subject is asked to put a check mark under each individual's name to which this construct can be applied.[9] If the construct cannot be applied to an individual, the space is left blank. This process is repeated 15 to 20 times or more but with different groupings. The result of this involved procedure is a rectangle with a series of voids (blanks) and checks with a list of constructs at the right-hand column. Grid data can then be subjected to numerous types of analysis.

The major analytical technique for examining grid measures of structure, within the framework of Kelly's theory, is the original non-parametric form of factor analysis proposed and devised by Kelly [43]. This technique was later revised and adapted to computer analysis by J. V. Kelly [45] The degree of differentiation was defined as the amount of variance not explained by the first factor [39].

Bieri has modified the Reptest developed by Kelly so that the instrument is more easily administered. Table 1 represents the modified Reptest of Bieri. The 10 roles are selected on the basis of being meaningful to an individual and are provided by the experimenter rather than elicited from the subject as is done in Kelly's procedure. A subject

---

[9] A more detailed description of the Reptest can be found in Kelly [44, Vol. 1], Bonarius [19, pp. 2-3], and Bannister and Mair [7, pp. 38-77].

rates each of the 10 persons on a scale of +3 to -3. No neutral point is provided.

An index of differentiation is derived from the modified Reptest through a matching procedure devised by Bieri [14, p. 7; 17, p. 190]. Once the subject has rated each role person on every bipolar construct, each row of ratings is compared to the rows below it. In the comparison of any two rows, when there is an exact agreement in the rating of a role person, a score of 1 is given. For example, in the role person "yourself" shown on Table 1, if you have ratings of +3 for both "outgoing" and "adjusted," then a score of 1 is given for that agreement. After making all possible comparisons between rows one and two, rows one and three are then compared with the resulting number of agreements marked down. This matching procedure is continued for all possible row comparisons.

After all comparisons are made, then the scores for each match are added so that you arrive at one score. In a 10 x 10 matrix, since there are 45 possible row comparisons within a column (role person) and 10 rows, there is a total possible differentiation score of 450. An individual with a score of 450 is assumed to have an undifferentiated cognitive system in that the construct dimensions were used in a functionally similar and homogeneous manner to construe the people on the grid. Those subjects with a score of 100 for example would be _relatively_ more differentiated because constructs were used differently in discriminating among the role persons. In other words, there is an inverse relationship between degree of differentiation and score of the modified Reptest.

As discussed above, Bieri has modified Kelly's Reptest in three main ways. In the first place, Bieri does not have the subjects elicit the constructs as does Kelly. He provides the constructs which are then rated. The second modification centers around the rating method for the Reptest. Bieri has each subject rank each role person on a +3 to -3 scale along each construct while Kelly has the subject use a checkmark if the construct applies to other role persons. Finally, Bieri's matching procedure is different from Kelly's procedure for scoring differentiation

Each of the Bieri modifications has been examined empirically in order to ascertain what effect they have had on the predictive efficacy of Kelly's formulation. Tripodi and Bieri [82] and Jaspers [39] examined the differences between differentiation scores when constructs are provided or are elicited. Both found that there are highly significant correlations between Bieri's procedure (provided constructs) and the one by Kelly (elicited constructs). In terms of Bieri's modification of scoring the Reptest grid, Bieri [17] reports a +.90 correlation between J. V. Kelly's [45] non-parametric factor analysis technique and his matching procedure where the scales were reduced to two, rather than six categories. These modifications thus do not appear to significantly alter the results from Kelly's Reptest on scoring and analyzing the structural aspects of the constructs.

Bieri's conceptualization of differentiation and subsequent measurement of it has been utilized in a number of psychological areas. Examples of the various areas include stimulus affect and perception [38, 53], social concept attainment [58], certainty of judgments made by individuals [83], and information transmission using both clinical and social stimuli [17].

The test-retest reliability of Bieri's technique is quite satisfactory. Tripodi and Bieri [82] had test-retest reliability coefficients of .86 when differentiation was based on an individual using constructs provided by the experimenter and .71 when based on constructs elicited from the subject. In other studies, the test-retest coefficients have been .70 [83] and .71 [84]. Epting [28], while analyzing three Bieri grids with social issues rather than role persons, found the test-retest reliability coefficients to range from 51 to .65.

The theory and operationalization of cognitive differentiation that will be used in this study is that proposed by Bieri [13, 14, 15, 16, 17]. Bieri's conceptualization of differentiation has been selected over that of Scott, Crockett, and others for several major reasons. First, while other major complexity theorists have also discussed differentiation, their emphasis has primarily been on integration [e.g., 36, 65]. Second, Bieri's concept of differentiation, being founded extensively on the work of Kelly [44], has a strong theoretical foundation. Third, Bieri's measurement technique has been shown to be applicable to a number of cognitive domains when appropriate modifications are made. Finally, there is no assumption that the attributes used by an individual to construe his world are dichotomous. Rather, a six-point scale is used to reflect that the construing of an object, along a dimension, is not necessarily black or white but rather some shade of gray. The Bieri approach to measuring differentiation, therefore, is conceptually closer to measuring attitude, via the Fishbein model, than is the sorting procedure by Scott [71], the essay analysis of Crockett [24], or other various techniques [e.g., 36, 91, 93].

Generalizability of Cognitive Differentiation Across Content Domains

A number of differentiation theorists have empirically examined whether the construct, cognitive differentiation, is generalizable across different domains.[10] If an individual who is relatively differentiated in one cognitive

---

[10]The emphasis is placed on the generalizability across different content areas when the same measurement instrument is being used.

domain is also relatively differentiated in other domains, then the usefulness of the concept to marketing practitioners is greater than if differentiation is domain specific.

It is Crockett's hypothesis that "individuals with complex cognitive systems with respect to other people need not necessarily have complex systems with respect to other domains" [24, p. 54] In one unpublished study, Crockett [24] reported that there is some degree of generality of differentiation within a given domain (people). No direct examination of the generalizability across distinct domains was presented.

Bieri [13, 15] emphasizes that the concept of differentiation is only applicable to an individual's social world. In fact, Bieri has stated that cognitive differentiation is concerned only with the dimensional versatility of a person in his social judgments [12]. There is no theoretical base, however, to support this contention since the concept of cognitive structure is theoretically applicable to physical as well as social stimuli. Moreover, Kelly, in an extensive discussion on the nature of the grid method, argues that since the construing process is applicable to all events, the grid method is generalizable [44, pp. 301-2].

In two different studies, Epting [27, 28] examined the generalizability question using the Bieri modification of the Reptest. The first study [27] examined the correlation between Bieri's traditional measure with role persons and related constructs and a modified measure designed to ascertain the level of social issue differentiation. The social issues ranged from "allowing Red China to become a member of the United Nations" to "abolishing the death sentence." The correlation between the two grids, although significant at the .05 level, was relatively low with a coefficient of .39. In a more recent study, Epting [28] developed three different Bieri grids to assess differentiation on three different sets of social issues. The correlation between the differentiation scores obtained from these grids ranged between .56 to .60.[11] Although it can be argued that the three areas used by Epting do not constitute completely independent content domains, the results certainly provide some evidence for the generalizability of differentiation.

Allard and Carlson [3] provide a more direct analysis of the generalizability proposition. They used Kelly's Reptest procedure and designed three grids which encompassed famous figures, geometric designs, and the person roles which Kelly used on his original instrument. The intercorrelations among the three measures of differentiation ranged from .57 to .67, all significant at the .001 level.

---

[11]Epting reports that he administered the grids twice to each respondent. The correlations presented here are those derived from the first administration.

Scott [72] has summarized a number of studies performed both by his students and by himself dealing with this question of generalizability. One specific section reported in his paper deals with the domain specificity versus generality of the various structural constructs developed by him. In his examination, Scott formed a composite score of various techniques to measure differentiation and then compared them across domains. The domains included acquaintances, family, groups, nations, school, and self. In order to examine the proposition of generalizability, the results of three different samples were presented. The mean interdomain correlation for a Boulder, Colorado, sample was .72 (6 domains), .66 for a sample of students at Kyoto, Japan (4 domains), and 58 for students at Wellington (2 domains). Based on these results, Scott concludes that a person's score on a differentiation variable is not dependent, necessarily, on the content area assessed. Because the scores reported were composites, this conclusion is not as strong as it might have been had the analysis dealt with individual measures of differentiation across domains.

The findings reported above, although not providing overwhelming support for the hypothesis that differentiation is generalizable across content areas, certainly do not refute it. In fact, the evidence is weighted more heavily in favor of generalizability than against it. The diversity of previous findings suggests then that additional studies encompassing dissimilar domains are needed before a definitive conclusion can be drawn regarding the generalizability issue.

CHAPTER III

RESEARCH HYPOTHESES

Before discussing the questions to be investigated in this study, a few of the major theoretical points concerning Fishbein's attitude theory and the concept of cognitive differentiation are reiterated.

Fishbein emphasizes that the concept of saliency of beliefs is a crucial one in the predictive efficacy of the attitude model. The conventional operationalization of the attitude model, however, assumes that the cognitive structure of each individual is composed of the same number of salient beliefs from which an attitude is formed. This assumption is inherent in the operationalization because typically a standard set of belief and evaluative statements is provided to each subject from which a predicted attitude score is abstracted. When the proportion of salient to total beliefs included in the standard set of evaluative statements is higher, the predictive validity of the Fishbein model is expected to be greater.

The concept of differentiation points out that attitudes concerning a range of stimuli in a product category can be based on few or many units of information and that this range varies from individual-to-individual [65, p 7]. Interpreting these units of information in an attitudinal framework as cognitive elements suggests that by taking cognitive differentiation into consideration a more appropriate number of cognitive elements may be used in the measurement of attitude. To the extent that an individual is highly differentiated in a given cognitive domain, the inclusion of a greater number of cognitive elements may improve the predicted measure of attitude. Conversely, if an individual is relatively undifferentiated, the predictive validity of the model may be higher when only the few salient dimensions are used.

A final theoretical area applies to the generalizability of cognitive differentiation across cognitive areas. If differentiation is generalizable across different product domains, the concept's applicability and use in marketing will be greatly facilitated compared to what would be the case if the concept is domain or product specific.

The research questions examined in this study are expressed in the alternative (H_a) and null (H_o) forms of the hypotheses presented below.

Hypothesis 1

H_a: There is a positive relationship between cognitive differentiation and the optimal number of cognitive elements used in the Fishbein attitude model to predict a given attitude.

H_o: There is no relationship between cognitive differentiation and the optimal number of cognitive elements used in the Fishbein attitude model to predict a given attitude.

Hypothesis 2

H_a: The predictive efficacy of the Fishbein attitude model is greater when an intra-individual analytic approach is used, where the number and entrance order of cognitive elements included in the model is allowed to vary for each individual, than when a cross-sectional procedure is utilized, where the respondents are aggregated and the number and entrance order remain the same.

H_o: The predictive efficacy of the Fishbein attitude model is not affected when an intra-individual analytic approach is used, where the number and entrance order of cognitive elements included in the model is allowed to vary, than when a cross-sectional procedure is utilized, where the respondents are aggregated and the number and entrance order remain the same.

Hypothesis 3

H_a: Cognitive differentiation is generalizable across two distinct product categories, one high involvement product category and one low involvement category, and interpersonal relations.

H_o: Cognitive differentiation is not generalizable across the two distinct product categories studied and interpersonal relations.

Each of these hypotheses is discussed in greater detail in the subsequent section describing the operationalization and analysis of the hypotheses.

Marketing Implications

If the null hypotheses are rejected in favor of the alternate ones, this study holds implications for the academician studying consumer behavior as well as the marketing practitioner.

Analysis of hypothesis 1 will provide insight into whether or not cognitive differentiation, a structural variable of cognition, influences the number of dimensions or cognitive elements that provide the best prediction of attitudes. This information will provide greater insight into how attitudes are developed, how they can be changed, and how to more effectively measure and predict them. Furthermore, assuming a positive relationship between cognitive and the number of optimal elements entered into the attitude model, a decision rule can be developed in terms of how many cognitive elements to include in the attitude model.

The first step in using this research, if hypothesis 1 is supported, is to determine if cognitive differentiation is linked to easily identifiable variables. Linking cognitive differentiation to these variables provides the marketing practitioner with the basis for identifying segments of the market who are differentiated and those who are not. Different marketing programs and strategies can then be directed at the relevant target market.

An individual who is cognitively differentiated, for example, may require more information along more product attributes for a change in attitude to occur than will the less differentiated individual. If differentiated individuals are the target market for a particular product, the marketing practitioner would realize that greater emphasis must be placed on the dissemination of product information to those individuals than may normally be required. In other words, greater emphasis would have to be placed on the promotional program with a resulting increase in promotional expenditures. If, on the other hand, the cost of providing additional information becomes prohibitive, a company might do well in aiming only at a less differentiated segment of consumers when an attitude change strategy is deemed necessary. In either instance, knowing the differentiation level for the target market should aid the practitioner in improving the impact of a promotional program by providing insight into the amount of information required.

With respect to hypothesis 2, if an intra-individual analytic procedure is found to be superior in predicting attitude, its use should provide greater confidence in using attitude models for developing and improving marketing strategies. This is important both for the academic researcher and the marketing practitioner.

If the concept of cognitive differentiation is generalizable across different cognitive domains (hypothesis 3), the use of cognitive differentiation would be greatly facilitated. An academic researcher or marketing practitioner would not have to be concerned with whether or not the influence of cognitive differentiation deviates between different product categories. Rather, they would realize, for example, that regardless of the product category more information is needed for a differentiated consumer than for an undifferentiated one.

CHAPTER IV

METHODOLOGY

Research Design

Product Selection

Two products were selected as focal points of this study. In light of the generalizability hypothesis (hypothesis 3), the two products were selected primarily on the basis of representing two distinct product categories. The criteria used for the selection of one product category were as follows: low unit price, purchased relatively frequently, low risk decision, and where peer group pressure would be minimal. In purchasing a brand in this product category, the level of involvement in the decision-making process would be expected to be relatively low. The criteria for the second product category were as follows: high unit price, purchased on an infrequent basis, high risk decision, and where peer group pressure would be expected to play a role in brand selection. A relatively high degree of involvement in the decision-making process would be expected for this product category. Use of such distinct product categories permitted an examination into whether differentiation is generalizable. In both cases, the product categories had to be ones in which consumers hold attitudes which they can reasonably express.

Two product categories which fit the above criteria are automobiles and toothpaste. An automobile is a highly visible and high risk decision whereas the type of toothpaste purchased has little social visibility and financial risk. Most people, including those respondents who participated in this study, hold attitudes and beliefs about the various brands within each product category and should be able to express them.

Sample Selection

The sample consisted of 102 undergraduate males enrolled in the College of Business and Administration at Southern Illinois University at Carbondale. Males were selected so that differences between attitudes and variations in differentiation due to sex would not be introduced into the data.

A convenience sample rather than a random procedure was employed due to length of the questionnaire. To avoid respondent non-interest and boredom which might result in haphazard responses, each respondent who completed the questionnaire was paid $3. Since the purpose of the study was to examine the theoretical relationship between differentiation and attitudes and not an attempt to generalize to a larger population, the use of students and a convenience sample was not viewed as a limiting factor.

Instrument Design

Eleven instruments were utilized in collecting the data necessary to test the three hypotheses set forth previously. They included a measure of (1) beliefs about the toothpaste brands (Fishbein's B_1 measure), (2) the evaluative aspect of the beliefs about toothpaste brands (Fishbein's a_1 measure), (3) attitudes towards the toothpaste brands, (4) differentiation measure for toothpaste, (5) determinism measure for toothpaste, (6) beliefs about the automobile brands (Fishbein's B_1 measure), (7) the evaluative aspect of the beliefs about automobile brands (Fishbein's B_1 measure), (8) attitudes toward automobile brands, (9) differentiation measure for automobiles, (10) determinism measure for automobiles, and (11) differentiation measure for interpersonal relations.

To develop these measures, two preliminary pretests were administered for each product category. Following Kaplan and Fishbein [40], an unstructured, free-recall questionnaire was presented to 73 male students in order to elicit the salient attributes and the relevant brands to be included later in the research questionnaire. The respondents had three minutes to answer each question. The free-recall questions for toothpaste and automobiles were:

1. Please <u>list</u> what you believe to be the characteristics and attributes of toothpastes

2. Please <u>list</u> the brands of toothpaste that you can recall.

3. Please <u>list</u> what you believe to be the characteristics and attributes of automobiles (with standard equipment) within the $2300 to $3500 price range.

4. Please <u>list</u> the brands of automobiles (with standard equipment) that you believe fall within a $2300 to $3500 price range.

The resulting list of salient attributes for toothpaste, which was included in the final research questionnaire, is presented in Table 2 along with the percentage of times each attribute was elicited. The frequency with which each attribute was elicited ranged from a minimum of 26.4% for price to a high of 68.1% for taste/flavor. It is interesting to note that a majority of these attributes have also been included in other marketing related studies [e.g., 10, 23].

TABLE 2

ATTRIBUTES ELICITED FOR TOOTHPASTE

Attributes	Percentage of Times Elicited
taste/flavor	68.1%
fresnen breath	62.5
cavity prevention	54.2
clean teeth	45.8
whiten/brighten[a]	37.5
texture	31.9
color	30.6
price	26.4

[a] Over 50% of the respondents who said whiten/brighten also included clean teeth, so the two attributes were deemed to be different on an a priori basis.

Eight brands of toothpaste were selected for inclusion on the basis of question 2 above. These brands were Close-up, Colgate, Crest, Gleem II, McClean's, Pearl Drops, Pepsodent, and Ultra Brite. Each brand was mentioned a minimum of 20 times (28%) and is a well-advertised national brand with differing advertising appeals.

Table 3 shows the salient attributes for automobiles and the percentage of time each was elicited in the preliminary pretest. Each attribute was elicited by a minimum of approximately 18% of the respondents, in the case of handling, and reached a high of 50.7% for gas mileage. Again, many of these attributes have been used in other attitude studies [e.g., 51].

TABLE 3

ATTRIBUTES ELICITED FOR AUTOMOBILES

Attributes	Percentage of Times Elicited
gas mileage	50.7%
economy	35.6
size	35.6
dependability	35.6
quality	30.1
style	24.7
performance	23.3
comfort	21.9
luxury	19.2
handling	17.8

In an attempt to ascertain what influence the "price restriction" in question 3 had on the attribute elicitation procedure, a follow-up study was employed. The same question without any price restriction was administered to essentially the same respondents two weeks after the first one. A Spearman rank correlation coefficient of .76 ($p < .01$) was found for the two series of attributes ranked according to the number of times each was mentioned. The major difference between the two was price. Price was ranked eleventh with seven respondents mentioning it in the "price restriction" questionnaire compared to seventh with 23 respondents when no price restriction was given.

In the final research questionnaire the price restriction was used so that the attributes associated with the brands would be more homogenous. The concern was that the attributes might not be stable or might differ between high priced prestigious automobiles and those automobiles which college students are more likely to purchase. Therefore, by including only those brands in the relevant price range this potential problem was circumvented.

Ten makes of automobiles were selected for inclusion in the questionnaire. They were VW Beetle, Cutlass, Dart, Javelin, Maverick, Mustang II, Pinto, Nova, Road Runner, and Vega. These makes were included due to their familiarity to the subjects, as indicated by question 4, and because they represented several major automobile manufacturers with a wide variety of prices and images within the price range of interest. In other words, these 10 automobile makes provided a representative sample of those available in the relevant price range. The number of makes was limited to 10 so that the size of the questionnaire would not be unwieldly or create undue respondent fatigue.

After these preliminary pretests were completed, the final questionnaire was developed. Form A in Appendix I-A shows the Fishbein differentiation, determinism, and attitude measures for toothpaste. Form B includes the same for automobiles (Appendix I-B).

The belief statements (B_i scale) for both product categories was a seven-point scale ranging from -3 to +3 indicating the probability that a given product attribute (e.g., freshen breath for toothpaste) is associated with a brand (e.g., Crest). The evaluative aspect of the beliefs (a_i) was also a seven point scale which ranged from -3 to +3. This component indicates the respondent's evaluation of the product attribute from bad (-3) to good (+3) regardless of the specific brand.

The attitudes toward each brand of automobile and toothpaste was measured in terms of as unidimensional measure of affect similar to that used by Bither and Miller [18], Klippel [47], and Mazis and Klippel [51]. This measure was a seven-point scale for each brand with one pole labeled "extremely low appeal" and the opposite pole "extremely high appeal."

Determinism scores for each attribute were ascertained by Alpert's [5, 55] "Dual Questioning Method," The information for this procedure was collected for use in determining the entry order of the cognitive elements into the predictive equation of the attitude model.[1] In the "Dual Questioning Method" two questions concerning each product attribute were asked. First the subjects were asked how important each attribute was in selecting a product and, secondly, whether they felt there were many differences between brands on that attribute. According to this procedure an attribute would not be considered a determinant attribute, even though it might be rated as extremely important if no differences were perceived between the respective brands.

Bieri's Reptest was used to measure cognitive differentiation for both product categories and interpersonal relations. For automobiles the Reptest was comprised of a 10 x 10 matrix with brand names and product attributes substituted for role persons and personal constructs. In the case of toothpaste the matrix was 8 x 8 and again the brand names and attributes replaced the interpersonal elements in the instrument.

---

[1]In addition to the determinism approach of ordering the entry of the cognitive elements into the equation, other methods were also employed. Each of the entrance procedures and the relevance of the entry order is discussed under hypothesis 1 in the Hypothesis Operationalization and Analysis section.

Essentially the same brands and product attributes contained in the attitude instruments were used in the Reptests because they were operationally defined as salient in the free elicitation procedure for attitudes. These brands and attributes should provide a more valid measure of differentiation than if non-salient attributes or brands were included. The product attributes, however, were not couched in the same terminology as those in the attitude model.

Cognitive differentiation is a measure of the respondent's ability to discriminate between brands on the amount of a given attribute present in each brand. Therefore, the Reptests presented asked <u>how</u> <u>much</u> of an attribute does a given brand contain. A value of +3 indicates the brand contains very much of the attribute and a -3 value indicates the brand does not contain the attribute. No neutral point is provided. The Fishbein attitude model, on the other hand, is interested in the <u>probability</u> or likelihood that a relationship exists between a product attribute, regardless of the level of the attribute, and a given brand and whether possessing that attribute is good or bad (the evaluative dimension). The use of these two instruments, while measuring two different things, facilitates the comparison between the two psychological concepts of attitude measurement and cognitive differentiation more than some other measure of differentiation such as that developed by Scott [71].[2]

The bipolar extremes used in Reptests were elicited in a fashion similar to that developed by Ahtola [1]. For automobiles (Appendix I-B, Form B) and toothpaste (Appendix I-A, Form A), the respondents were asked to describe the brands of toothpaste and automobiles with respect to several characteristics. Furthermore, they were asked to describe the brands only in terms of characteristics and not in terms of their preference. These questionnaires were administered to the same respondents one month after the original salient attributes were elicited. The bipolar extremes selected were those elicited most by the respondents.

The only modification to the original Bieri Reptest (Appendix I-C) for interpersonal relations used in this study was the substitution of "instructor" for "boss" as a role person. Since a substantial proportion of students had not held a full-time job for a period longer than two months of summer employment, a change was deemed necessary because they had little work experience on which to rely in differentiating "boss" from other roles. Both the original and modified Reptests were 10 x 10 matrices with 10 role persons and 10 bipolar constructs.

---

[2] Scott's method of measuring differentiation was presented earlier in the discussions under the heading Cognitive Differentiation: Measurement and Meaning.

In administering the questionnaire, half of the respondents were asked to complete Form A (toothpaste) first and half Form B (automobiles). This was done to minimize any systematic biases which might occur by having all respondents answer one of the forms first. The Reptest for interpersonal relations was last in each instance. The presentation order of the various brands and attributes was varied in a random fashion and all brands were rated within attributes, i.e., the brands were rated for each attribute rather than rating each brand along all attributes. These precautions were taken in an attempt to reduce any possible halo effect by reducing the opportunity to compare the responses with prior ratings [86].

The parts of the questionnaire pertaining to Fishbein's belief statements (B_i) and the Reptest were separated by other instruments to minimize any possible perceived similarity between the measures and resulting respondent confusion. The instructions and operations were also quite different. The order of the various measures in Forms A and B was as follows: (1) the evaluative aspects of the beliefs, (2) belief statements, (3) attitudes toward brands, (4) importance measure for the determinism score, (5) difference measure for the determinism score, and (6) differentiation measure.

Instrument Pretest

A pretest was conducted in order to ascertain whether the instructions were clear and therefore elicited the appropriate responses and if the time necessary to complete the questionnaire was reasonable. Five College of Business and Administration male students from Southern Illinois University at Carbondale volunteered and were compensated for participating in the pretest. Following the completion of the questionnaire, each respondent was asked to express, in his own words, why he responded the way he did to each set of questions. Furthermore, each respondent was asked to indicate if any questions and instructions were not clear and, if so, how they could be improved. Each of these respondents came from the same population as those who participated in the final study.

Only minor modifications were necessary because it appeared that the respondents had no difficulty in comprehending the questions and were answering them properly. The time required to complete the questionnaire ranged from 22 to 45 minutes with only one individual taking more than 40 minutes.

Hypothesis Operationalization and Analysis

The purpose of this section is to describe the statistical procedures employed in examining the three research hypotheses. In each instance the alternative form of the hypothesis is presented and operationally defined, followed by discussion of the statistical methodology.

Hypothesis 1: Cognitive Differentiation and the Number of Cognitive Elements

A respondent's cognitive differentiation score, based on a modification of the Bieri Reptest (see Chapter IV) constitutes the predictor (independent variable) variable in hypothesis 1. The optimal number of cognitive elements used for predicting a given attitude represents the criterion (dependent variable). Cognitive elements are defined as the $B_i a_i$ components in the Fishbein attitude model. The "optimal" number of such elements is operationally defined as the number yielding the best correlation between the elicited and predicted ($\sum_{i=1}^{n} B_i a_i$) measures of attitude. What constitutes the best correlation is based on six separate criteria which are described in subsequent paragraphs.

The alternative form of the hypothesis states that there is a positive relationship between cognitive differentiation and the optimal number of cognitive elements used in the Fishbein attitude model to predict a given attitude. A low score derived from the Reptest indicates a high degree of differentiation whereas a high score indicates a low degree of differentiation. Therefore, the alternative form of the research hypothesis suggests a negative correlation between the cognitive differentiation score and the optimal number of cognitive elements for the Fishbein model.

The examination of this relationship requires two stages of analysis. The first involves ascertaining the optimal number of cognitive elements to include in the equation for predicting an attitude and the second involves correlating this number with the differentiation score.

To determine the optimal number of cognitive elements, each of the elements was introduced into the equation one at a time, according to a specified entry criterion, until all of the elements were included. Each time another element was added, the elicited attitude toward the brands was correlated to the predicted attitude. This entrance procedure is shown in Figure 1 in flow chart form for automobiles.[3]

For the purpose of this study, six entrance criteria or decision rules were used in defining the optimal number of cognitive elements because no single criteria was without possible limitations. The entrance criteria, with one exception, were applied in two ways. In one, the entrance order of the cognitive elements was permitted to vary between individuals. In the second, the entrance order of the cognitive elements remained stable across all respondents.

---

[3]This staged entrance procedure is similar to that used by Willie and Weinreich [88]

FIGURE 1

STAGED ENTRANCE PROCEDURE

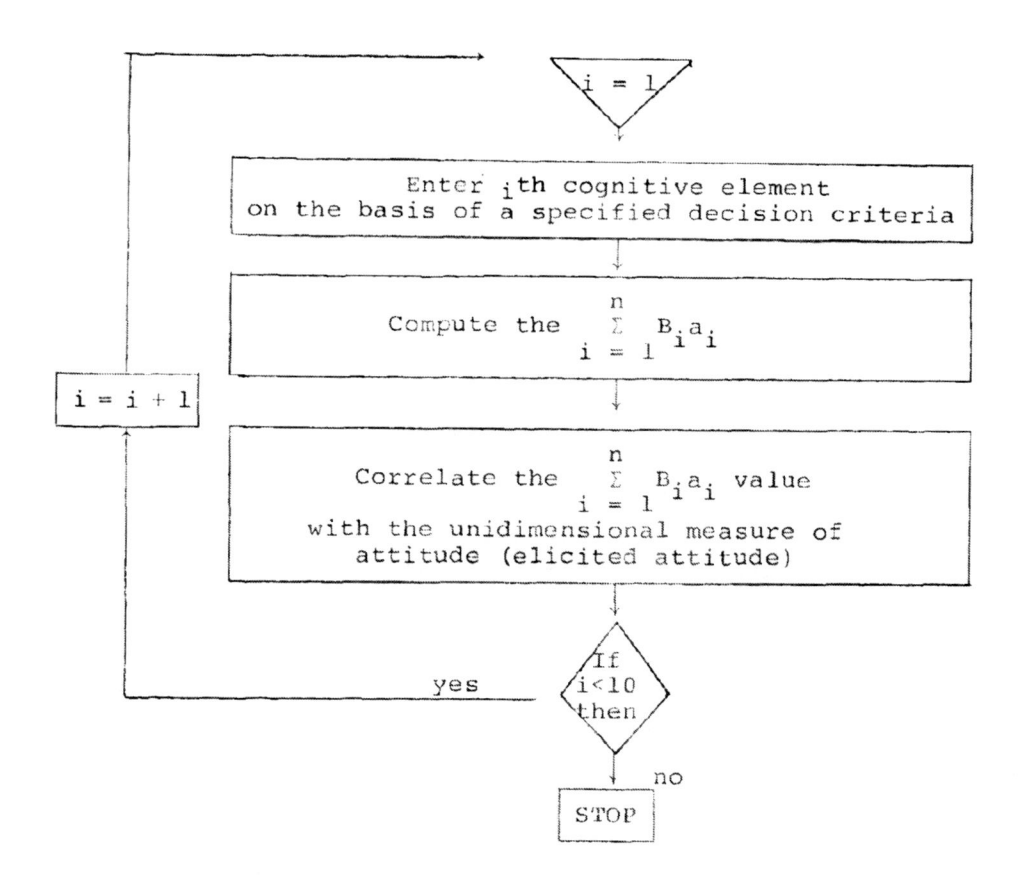

```
            ┌──────────────────┐
            │      i = 1       │
            └────────┬─────────┘
                     ▼
    ┌────────────────────────────────────────────┐
    │      Enter ith cognitive element           │
    │ on the basis of a specified decision criteria │
    └────────────────────┬───────────────────────┘
                         ▼
    ┌────────────────────────────────────────────┐
    │                    n                       │
    │   Compute the     Σ   B_i a_i              │
    │                  i = 1                     │
    └────────────────────┬───────────────────────┘
                         ▼
    ┌────────────────────────────────────────────┐
    │                       n                    │
    │   Correlate the      Σ   B_i a_i   value   │
    │                     i = 1                  │
    │   with the unidimensional measure of       │
    │        attitude (elicited attitude)        │
    └────────────────────┬───────────────────────┘
                         ▼
                    ╱ If   ╲
             yes   ╱ i<10   ╲
        ◄────────╲ then    ╱
                  ╲        ╱
                     │ no
                     ▼
                   STOP
```

$i = 1$

$\sum_{i=1}^{n} B_i a_i$

$i = i + 1$

For example, in the first way cognitive element number two might enter into the predictive equation first for respondent five but fifth for respondent 20. In the second way, the cognitive element would be entered into the equation in the same order for both respondents.

The concern was to utilize several criteria to guard against accepting or rejecting the hypotheses based on results that might be influenced by choice of entrance criteria. At the same time, however, they were similar enough to permit a comparison of the results across the various entrance criteria.

The six basic criteria were

1. Peak Salience
2. Peak Determinism
3. Peak Regression
4. Significant Salience
5. Significant Determinism
6. Significant Regression.

The first three measures are labeled "peak" because the number of optimal elements, subsequently compared with the differentiation scores, was simply that which provides the highest absolute correlation coefficient between the elicited and predicted attitude measures. This is an approach similar to that used by Wilkie and Weinreich [88], which does not take into consideration whether the addition of one more cognitive element increases the predictive efficacy of the model significantly. Using a peak approach, if the addition of one element increased the correlation from 58 to .59 between the elicited and predicted attitude measures, then that number of cognitive elements would be used even though the .01 increase may in fact be meaningless.

The last three measures labeled "significant," however, take into consideration whether the addition of a cognitive element increases the correlation coefficient significantly. These latter measures decrease the likelihood that the number of elements included in the analysis is the result of a spurious and insignificant increase in the correlation coefficient.

As elements are added to the equation, the correlation coefficient may either increase or decrease. Hence a number of "peaks" may exist as illustrated in Figure 2. The "significant" designation pertains to the number of cognitive elements producting the highest correlation coefficient that is significantly greater, in a statistical sense, than the next lowest coefficient.

To determine the optimal significant number of elements to be included in the next stage of analysis, the correlation coefficients corresponding to various numbers of cognitive elements in the attitude model were compared. For example, point b in Figure 2 would first be compared to point a. If point b was significantly higher, then c would be compared to point b, and so on. In this illustration, if c was higher than b, but d was not significantly higher than c, the number of cognitive elements subsequently analyzed in relation to differentiation would be 4.

FIGURE 2

PLOT OF CORRELATION COEFFICIENTS BETWEEN
THE PREDICTED AND ELICITED ATTITUDE AS
THE NUMBER OF COGNITIVE ELEMENTS VARIES

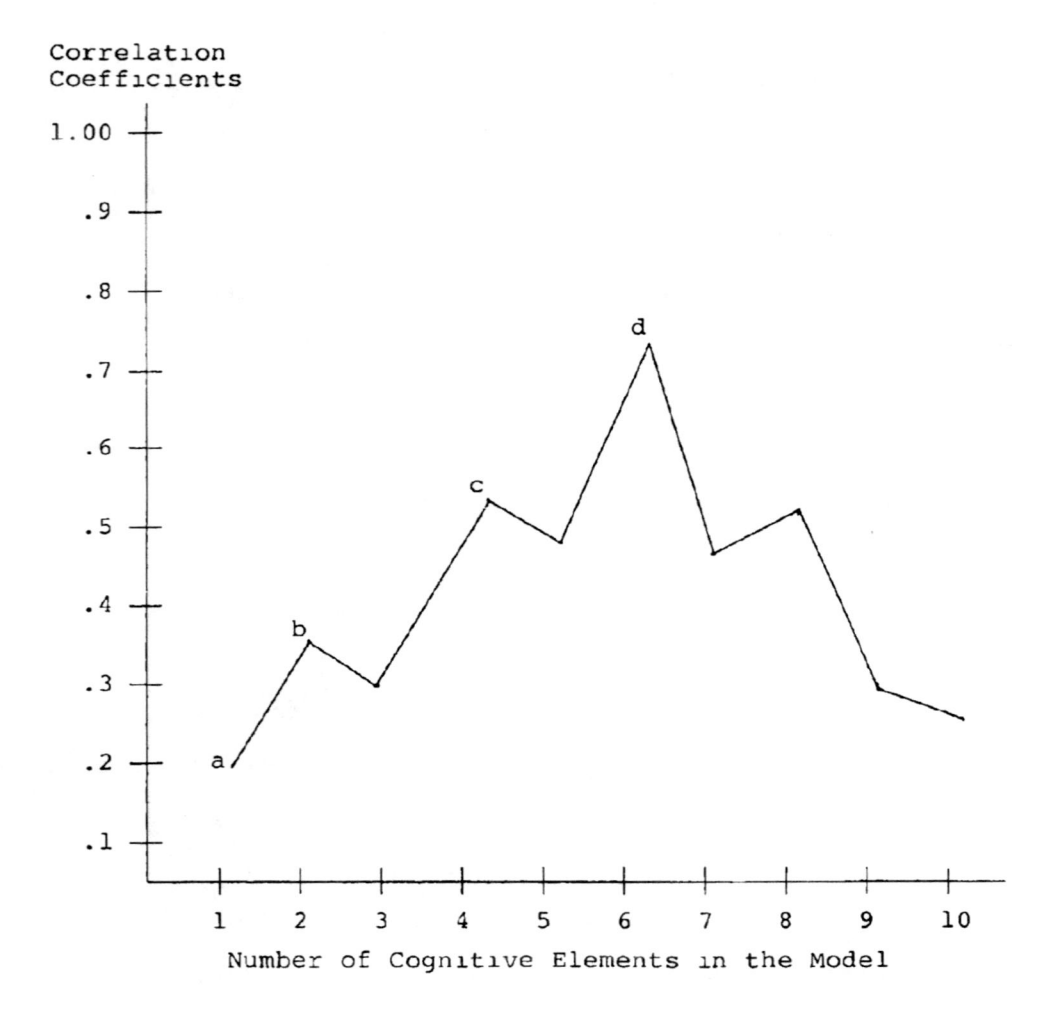

The formula, used for comparing the various r's, was developed by Hotelling and takes the form of a "t" test [34, p. 190]. This formula tests whether the r's are significantly different and takes into consideration the intercorrelation between the r's when the number (i) of cognitive elements included in the model is different. The formula is

$$t_{dr} = (r_{12} - r_{13}) \bigg/ \sqrt{\frac{(n-3)(1+r_{23})}{2(1 - r_{23}^2 - r_{12}^2 - r_{13}^2 + 2r_{23} r_{12} r_{13})}} \ ;$$

where

- r_{12} is the correlation between the elicited and predicted attitude at point i (e.g., when two elements are included),

- r_{13} is the correlation between the elicited and predicted attitude at point i + n (e.g., when three elements are included),

- r_{23} is the correlation between the predicted attitudes at point i and at point i + n, and

- n is the number of brands being evaluated in the equation (10 for automobiles and 8 for toothpaste).

The alpha level used to determine the significant level in the analysis was .35 for a one-tailed test. This alpha level was selected so as not to be so stringent as to eliminate legitimate increases in r but powerful enough to take into consideration only spurious increases. Since this analysis revolves around being able to reject the null hypothesis that the two peaks are equal when in fact they are different, a Type II error is of critical importance. Hence a large alpha level was selected which reduces beta (the probability of a Type II error).

The term "salience" applied to two of the entry criteria (peak and significant) means that the cognitive elements were entered into the predictive portion of the equation according to the saliency hierarchy. The hierarchy was operationalized as the number of times each attribute was elicited in the preliminary phase of the study. In the case of toothpaste, for example, since taste/flavor was elicited by 68.1% of those in the pretest it was entered into the model first, followed by freshen breath with 62.5% and so forth. The last cognitive element to be entered was price with 26.4% of the respondents eliciting the construct. The same approach was followed for automobiles.[4] Based on the operationalization of the salience procedure, the cognitive element entrance order did not vary between respondents.

The entrance procedure designated as "determinism" was based on a measure developed by Alpert [5, 55]. This measures the importance of each attribute and whether the respondent perceives differences among the brands with respect to that attribute. Although the attribute is very important, theoretically if there are no perceived differences aong the brands along the attribute, it would not be determinant in the formation of an attitude. Determinism score for each respondent was computed according to the formula

---

[4] The ordering of economy, size, and dependability of automobiles, since each was elicited the same number of time, were randomly assigned.

$$D_i = P_i \times I_i,$$

where

D_i is the determinism score for attribute i,

P_i is the perceived difference between brands along attribute i, and

I_i is the importance of attribute i.

The attribute with the highest mean determinism score was entered first, the one with the second highest mean score was entered second into the attitude model, and so forth. This procedure is similar to that of Wilkie and Weinreich [88] although they operationally defined P_i differently than did Alpert.[5]

When the entrance of the cognitive elements were allowed to vary on an intra-individual basis, the determinism score for each attribute for each individual was used. In the case where the entrance order remained the same across individuals, a mean determinism score for each attribute across respondents was computed.

The final entrance procedure is designated "regression." This approach was operationalized through the use

---

[5]Wilkie and Weinreich operationalized P_i by taking the standard deviation of the attribute ratings across stores rather than asking the respondents to state the extent to which they perceived differences among the stores along an attribute.

of a stepwise regression procedure, BMD02R [25].[6] In this procedure, the order of variable insertion into the regression equation followed the rank order of the partial correlation coefficients, beginning with the largest and concluding with the smallest. The partial correlation serves as a measure of the importance of each of the variables [26, p. 69] which follows conceptually the salience and determinism entrance procedures. The elicited measure of attitude was the criterion or dependent variable and the cognitive elements were the independent or predictor variables. The order in which the cognitive elements were inserted in the regression equation was the order followed in entering them into the predicted portion of the attitude model. This stepwise entrance procedure is an effective complement to the theoretically based determinism and saliency procedures.

Where the entrance order was allowed to vary from individual-to-individual, the stepwise procedure was applied to each individual to define the ordering for that individual. When the entrance order remained the same across all respondents, the stepwise procedure was applied to the aggregated sample to determine the element entry order.

---

[6] While the stepwise regression procedure may not provide an optimal solution, it is recommended over the other variable selection procedures by Draper and Smith [26, p. 172].

Once the optimal number of cognitive elements was ascertained for each entrance procedure the final stage in testing hypothesis 1 was completed. In this step the optimal number of cognitive elements, derived earlier, was correlated with the respondents' respective cognitive differentiation scores for toothpaste and automobiles. Ten correlation coefficients for each product category resulted for each of the two product categories, four correlation coefficients for the determinism and regression entrance procedures, and two for the salience procedure.[7]

Hypothesis 2. Predictive Efficacy of the Intra-Individual versus Cross-Sectional Analytic Procedures in the Attitude Model

The difference in the predictive efficacy of the Fishbein attitude model when two different analytic techniques are used is the focal point of this hypothesis. The alternative form of the hypothesis states that the predictive efficacy of the Fishbein attitude model is greater when an intra-individual analytic technique is used, where the number and entrance order of the cognitive elements included in the model are allowed to vary for each individual, than when a cross-sectional procedure is utilized, where the

---

[7] Again, the salience procedure did not permit the entrance order to vary between individuals based on the elicitation procedure. The entry order is the same regardless of whether or not the entry order is stable or is permitted to vary across individuals.

respondents are aggregated and the number and entrance order remain the same.

It should be noted at this juncture that there are two sources of variation in the predictive efficacy of the attitude model. One is the variation in the cognitive element entrance order. The second is the variation between individuals in the number of elements entered into the model.

In the operationalization of this hypothesis, predictive efficacy was defined as the correlation between the elicited and predicted measures of attitude. The intra-individual analytic approach required that each respondent be treated as a subsample in correlating the elicited and predicted measures of attitude. Hence, a correlation coefficient for each respondent resulted for each cognitive element entrance procedure (e.g., determinism, salience). In the case of the cross-sectional procedure, one correlation coefficient resulted for each of the cognitive element entrance approaches.

The correlation coefficients from the intra-individual and cross-sectional analysis were transformed using Fisher's r to Z procedure before the two sets of data were compared. This transformation was necessary, prior to a statistical comparison, because correlation coefficients have skewed distributions. In the absence of transformation, statistical tests comparing the mean correlation coefficients would not satisfy the normality assumption. The relationship of a correlation coefficient, r, to Fisher's Z, with Z approximately normally distributed with a variance of $\frac{1}{n-3}$, is [34, p. 163]

$$Z = 1/2 \left[\log_e (1 + r) - \log_e (1 - r)\right].$$

A series of $\bar{Z}$ tests were used to test the differences between the correlation coefficients derived from the cross-sectional analysis and the intra-individual approach. For each cognitive element entrance procedure, the Z score of the correlation coefficient derived from cross-sectional analysis was compared against the mean transformed Z scores derived from the intra-individual analysis. These tests were made using the formula [34, p. 190]

$$\bar{Z} = \frac{Z_1 - Z_2}{\sqrt{\frac{1}{n_1 - 3} \quad \frac{1}{n_2 - 3}}}$$

for two unmatched samples of Fisher Z's. A separate test was performed on the correlation coefficients arising from each cognitive element entrance procedure.

Hypothesis 3: Generalizability of Cognitive Differentiation

The acceptance or rejection of this hypothesis is based on the positive intercorrelation of the differentiation scores derived from three different cognitive domains. The hypothesis in alternative form states that cognitive differentiation is generalizable across two distinct product categories, one high involvement product category and one low involvement category, and interpersonal relations.

In operational terms, this hypothesis states that a person who exhibits a relatively high degree of differentiation will tend to have similar levels of differentiation in other domains. Those with low differentiation in a domain will tend to be low in others. The three cognitive domains, in this study, were automobiles, toothpaste, and interpersonal relations. The differentiation scores for each were derived from a Reptest.

CHAPTER V

RESULTS AND DISCUSSION

Hypothesis 1: Cognitive Differentiation and the Number of Cognitive Elements

In analyzing hypothesis 1, the results on toothpaste and automobiles will be presented separately. Once both sets of findings have been discussed a comparison of the findings will be made

Toothpaste

The optimal number of cognitive elements was positively related to cognitive differentiation in each of the six entrance procedures, as suggested by the alternative hypothesis. Whether the entrance order was permitted to vary between respondents or whether each element was entered in the same order across respondents did not influence the acceptance or rejection of the hypothesis. Only when the significant determinism entrance procedure was employed, however, was the relationship between cognitive differentiation and the optimal number of cognitive elements included in the attitude model significant at the .05 level. The correlation coefficient, as shown in Table 4, was -.31

TABLE 4

CORRELATIONS BETWEEN NUMBER OF COGNITIVE ELEMENTS
AND COGNITIVE DIFFERENTIATION SCORE FOR TOOTHPASTE

	Peak Determinism	Peak Regression	Peak Salience	Significant Determinism	Significant Regression	Significant Salience
Elements entered in same order	-.161	-.138	-.057	-.310[b]	-.040	-.074
Element order allowed to vary	-.181[a]	-.094	c	-.223[b]	-.068	c

[a] $p < .10$
[b] $p < .05$
[c] The salience procedure operationally does not permit the element entrance order to vary between respondents.

when the cognitive elements were entered in the same order and -.223 when the element order was allowed to vary between respondents. A negative sign resulted because a low numerical differentiation score stems from a relatively high degree of cognitive differentiation.

The remaining significant correlation coefficient, significant at the .10 level, existed in the case of the peak determinism entrance procedure when the entrance order of the cognitive elements was allowed to vary. None of the three correlation coefficients, even though they were significant at the .10 level or greater, have an r^2, amount of variance explained, greater than .10. These results provided only partial support for the hypothesis that a positive relationship exists between the optimal number of cognitive elements and cognitive differentiation and toothpaste. If the r^2's were larger or if significant relationships had been shown in other entrance procedures, then the alternative hypothesis could have been accepted.

It does not appear, furthermore, that allowing the cognitive elements to vary between respondents enlarged the correlation between differentiation and the optimal number of elements in the attitude model. The correlation coefficients within each entrance order procedure (elements allowed to vary versus elements in the same order) were not significantly different ($p<.05$) from one another. No pattern seemed to be present, in that for half of the entry methods the correlation coefficients were higher when the elements were entered in the same order and for the other half when the element order varied.

The coefficients presented in Table 4 were based on 99 respondents who were included in the toothpaste portion of the study. Three were discarded out of the 102 completed questionnaires because the correlation between the predicted and elicited measures of attitude was undefined. This was due to the absence of any variance between the cognitive elements in evaluating the eight brands of toothpaste.

Automobiles

The analysis yielded very little evidence that the optimal number of cognitive elements was significantly related to cognitive differentiation for automobiles. Although the signs of all but one of the correlation coefficients were in the predicted direction, the value of the coefficients shown in Table 5 (based on 102 respondents) were not significant at the .05 level. This statistical evidence dictated acceptance of the null hypothesis of no relationship between the optimal number of cognitive elements and cognitive differentiation for this product category.

TABLE 5

CORRELATIONS BETWEEN NUMBER OF COGNITIVE ELEMENTS
AND COGNITIVE DIFFERENTIATION SCORE FOR AUTOMOBILES

	Peak Determinism	Peak Regression	Peak Salience	Significant Determinism	Significant Regression	Significant Salience
Elements entered in same order	-.030	-.026	-.106	-.076	.024	-.021
Element order allowed to vary	-.088	-.008	a	-.042	-.021	a

[a] The salience procedure operationally does not permit the element entrance order to vary between respondents.

The results for toothpaste and automobiles, evaluated together, seemed to hint at some relationship between cognitive differentiation and the optimal number of cognitive elements. No element entrance approach, however, provided significant results both for toothpaste and automobiles. Only in the case of the significant determinism entrance procedure were significant correlations found for toothpaste. If other entrance procedures had produced significant results for toothpaste but not automobiles, one might argue that the relationship between cognitive differentiation and the optimal number of elements is product specific. Since this was not the case a strong relationship did not appear to exist between cognitive differentiation and the number of elements included in the model.

Hypothesis 2: Predictive Efficacy of the Intra-Individual versus Cross-Sectional Analytic Procedures in the Attitude Model

To test whether the predictive efficacy of the Fishbein attitude model is greater when the analysis is on an intra-individual basis than on a cross-sectional basis, correlations between the predicted and elicited attitude were calculated for each individual separately and for the sample as a whole. These two sets of correlation coefficients were then compared. The discussion of results will be separated on the basis of the two product categories examined.

Toothpaste

The coefficients for the cross-sectional (respondents aggregated for analysis) and the intra-individual (attitude model applied to each respondent individually) analyses (Table 6) were compared through a series of Z tests set out in Chapter IV. The mean correlation coefficients for the intra-individual analysis (99 respondents) were derived by transforming the original r's to Fisher's Z scores. Then the mean of the Z scores for each entrance procedure was computed. These Z scores were transformed into the r values which are shown in Table 6. These mean correlation coefficients were based on the distribution of coefficients derived for each respondent and are shown in Appendices II-A (elements allowed to vary) and B (elements entered in the same order).

In testing this hypothesis, the cross-sectional coefficient for the salience entrance procedure (.463 in Table 6), for example, was compared to the peak and significant salience coefficients (.751 and .735, respectively) derived from intra-individual analysis. Similar comparisons were made for the regression and determinism procedures' coefficients, resulting in a total of 10 tests for differences between coefficients corresponding to the cross-sectional and intra-individual analyses for each procedure.

TABLE 6

CORRELATION COEFFICIENTS DERIVED FROM INTRA-INDIVIDUAL
AND CROSS-SECTIONAL ANALYSES FOR TOOTHPASTE (n=99)

	Peak Determinism	Peak Regression	Peak Salience	Significant Determinism	Significant Regression	Significant Salience
Intra-Individual						
Elements entered in same order	.750	.788	.751	.756	.780	.735
Element order allowed to vary	.678	.813	a	.709	.814	a
Cross-Sectional	.463	.415	.521	b	b	b

[a] The salience procedure operationally did not permit the element entrance order to vary between respondents.

[b] The peak correlations were significantly higher than the next lowest ones in the cross-sectional analysis because of the large sample size. That is to say, the peak correlations were also the significant correlations.

In each of the 10 comparisons, the mean correlation for the intra-individual analytic approach was significantly greater (p<.05) than the correlation derived from the cross-sectional procedure. The null hypothesis, therefore, is rejected in favor of the alternative hypothesis which states that the predictive efficacy of the Fishbein attitude model is greater when an intra-individual analytic approach is used than when a cross-sectional procedure is implemented for toothpaste.

Automobiles

The coefficients for the cross-sectional and the intra-individual analytic procedures for automobiles (Table 7) were analyzed in the same fashion as for toothpaste. In each instance, the correlation of the cross-sectional analysis entrance procedure was compared to the appropriate intra-individual analysis correlation coefficients.

The intra-individual mean correlation coefficients were significantly greater (p<.05) than those coefficients derived from the cross-sectional analysis in all but one instance. The intra-individual analysis significant determinism correlation coefficient was significantly greater than the cross-sectional procedure at the .10, rather than the .05, level when the elements were entered in the same order for all respondents. These results

TABLE 7

CORRELATION COEFFICIENTS DERIVED FROM INTRA-INDIVIDUAL
AND CROSS-SECTIONAL ANALYSES FOR AUTOMOBILES (n=102)

	Peak Determinism	Peak Regression	Peak Salience	Significant Determinism	Significant Regression	Significant Salience
Intra-Individual						
Elements entered in same order	.738	.756	.816	.709	.754	.808
Element order allowed to vary	.775	.778	a	.738	.778	a
Cross-Sectional	.689	.597	.619	b	b	b

[a] The salience procedure operationally did not permit the element entrance order to vary between respondents.

[b] The peak correlations were significantly higher than the next lowest ones in the cross-sectional analysis because of the large sample size. That is to say, the peak correlations were also the significant correlations.

provided strong support for the rejection of the null hypothesis that the intra-individual approach does not improve the predictive efficacy of the attitude model over the cross-sectional approach for automobiles.

One possible explanation for the significant differences in the predictive efficacy of the Fishbein attitude model when the analysis proceeds on an intra-individual basis versus a cross-sectional one has been provided by Bass and Wilkie [11]. The argument posed by Bass and Wilkie is that normalization of the responses adjusts for within-subject variance in responses. This is necessary because different individuals may have different anchor points and response sets in evaluating brands and product attributes which would not be reflected in a cross-sectional analysis. Normalization of the responses, according to Bass and Wilkie, will eliminate this problem and increase the predictive efficacy of the attitude model when a cross-sectional analysis is used.

The formula proposed by Bass and Wilkie to normalize the belief (BN) of the $\underline{k}$th consumer of the $\underline{i}$th attribute for the $\underline{j}$th brand is [11, p. 265]

$$BN_{ijk} = B_{ijk}/\Sigma_j B_{ijk}.$$

Similarly the formula for normalizing the importance weight (IN) is [11, p. 265]

$$IN_{ik} = I_{jk}/\Sigma_i I_{ik}.$$

It should be noted that a modification of Fishbein's attitude model was employed in the Bass and Wilkie study where the belief and importance measures ranged from 1 to 7 rather than from -3 to +3 as in the case of the original Fishbein model. The Fishbein attitude model cannot be normalized in the Bass and Wilkie manner because of the way in which the components of the predicted attitude (B_i and a_i) are measured. Adding a negative response in the Fishbein model very likely reduced the denominator in the Bass and Wilkie formula and therefore artificially inflates the importance or belief measure.

One alternative to the above approach to normalizing the predicted measure of attitude for this study is to standardize the belief and evaluative components on the basis of Z scores. This standardization approach, unlike the one proposed by Bass and Wilkie, allows for negative and zero responses. The formula for standardizing the belief (B_i) of the <u>k</u>th consumer of the <u>i</u>th attribute for the <u>j</u>th brand is

$$Z_{ijk} = \frac{X_{ijk} - \bar{X}_{ik}}{\sigma_{ik}} ,$$

where

X_{ijk} is the response of the kth consumer on the ith attribute for the jth brand,

$\overline{X}_{ik}$ is the mean response of the kth consumer on the ith attribute across all brands, and

σ_{ik} is the standard deviation for the kth consumer on the ith attribute across all brands.

Similarly the formula for standardizing the evaluative component (a_i) is[1]

$$z_{ik} = \frac{X_{ik} - \overline{X}_k}{\sigma_k},$$

where

X_{ik} is the response of the kth consumer on the ith attribute,

$\overline{X}_k$ is the mean response of the kth consumer, and

σ_k is the standard deviation for the kth consumer across all attributes.

When the predicted and elicited measures of attitude in this study were standardized in the manner described above, the coefficients were lower than those based on the non-standardized data in all but one instance. The determinism entrance procedure for toothpaste was the only case in which the correlation coefficient was higher on the standardized data than on the non-standardized data (Table 8). The increase was not significant, however, at the .05 level.

---

[1] The elicited attitude was also standardized for each respondent across brands.

TABLE 8

CORRELATION COEFFICIENTS BASED ON STANDARDIZED AND NON-STANDARDIZED DATA FOR DIFFERENT ENTRANCE PROCEDURES--CROSS-SECTIONAL ANALYSIS

Entrance Procedure	Toothpaste Standardized	Non-Standardized[a]	Automobiles Standardized	Non-Standardized[a]
Salience	.397	.463	.391	.689
Determinism	.493	.415	.469	.597
Regression	.493	.521	.499	.619

[a]These non-standardized coefficients are the same as those presented in Tables 6 and 7 for toothpaste and automobiles, respectively.

Using the Fishbein attitude model employed in this study, it is apparent that standardizing the data does not improve the predictive ability of the cross-sectional approach over the intra-individual technique. A theoretical explanation for the apparent failure of the standardization process rests with the operationalization of the Fishbein model. The standardization process redefines the respondent's cognitive element in a fashion that is contrary to the Fishbein attitude theory. For example, assume that a respondent has an average belief rating for a Ford Pinto of -2 across five attributes. By standardizing the belief ratings, any belief rating of -1 would then become a positive Z score. Multiplying this positive Z score times a +2 rating on the evaluative scale (a_i) provides a cognitive element with a positive Z score rather than a negative cognitive element required by the attitude model.

In comparing the results from toothpaste and automobiles for both the non-standardized and standardized data, an additional comment needs to be made. For both the salience and determinism entrance procedures in the non-standardized cross-sectional analysis (Tables 6 and 7), the correlation coefficients for automobiles are significantly greater ($p < .05$) than for toothpaste. This difference is similar to findings of Mazis and Klippel [62] who observed substantial differences in correlations between automobiles, toothpaste, and mouthwash.

These significant differences in the predictive efficiency between automobiles and toothpaste were not found in the intra-individual analysis phase of this study. In no instance was the mean automobile correlation coefficient, between predicted and elicited attitude, significantly different ($p<.05$) than the toothpaste mean correlation coefficient for the same entrance procedure.

Bass and Talarzyk [10], when employing intra-individual analysis, also found few significant differences in the predictive efficiency of an attitude model between six different product categories. The probability of correctly predicting the most preferred brands was significantly different ($p<.05$) only between toothpaste and toilet tissue in their study.

The possibility of biases in anchor points and response sets in the cross-sectional approach offers one possible explanation why differences were found between automobiles and toothpaste in the case of cross-sectional analysis but not for the intra-individual procedure. The biases would not arise in the intra-individual procedure because the respondents are not aggregated. In other words, differences between the predictive efficacy of the attitude model between product categories might be an artifact of the analytic technique rather than an accurate representation of the respondents' cognitive systems.

It is interesting to note that allowing the entry order to vary among respondents did not produce systematically higher correlation coefficients for either product category. Stated differently, entering the elements in the same order using the intra-individual analytic procedure did not appear to systematically reduce the predictive efficacy of the attitude model. The expectation was that the correlation would be higher when the element order was allowed to vary for each individual because of individual differences in attribute salience. Having found no significant difference, an argument might be made for entering all elements in the same order since it makes the analysis easier and the results can be more easily interpreted for planning new marketing strategies.

Hypothesis 3: Generalizability of Cognitive Differentiation

The intercorrelations between the differentiation scores for the two product categories and interpersonal relations did not provide strong support for the hypothesis that cognitive differentiation is generalizable across the domains studied. In two of the three comparisons shown in Table 9, the correlation coefficients were significant at the .05 level. The correlation of the differentiation scores between toothpaste and interpersonal relations was significant at the .10 level. Although these coefficients were significant, the small amount of shared variance suggests that only a small degree of differentiation is generalizable across these three domains. Hence, the null hypothesis was not rejected.

TABLE 9

CORRELATION MATRIX BETWEEN DIFFERENTIATION
LEVELS FOR THREE COGNITIVE DOMAINS

Cognitive Domain	1	2	3
1. Toothpaste	1.000		
2. Automobiles	.3266[a]	1.000	
3. Interpersonal Relations	.1803[b]	.2168[a]	1.000

[a] $p < .05$
[b] $p < .10$

It is interesting to note that the correlation coefficient between automobiles and toothpaste, the two product categories used in this study, was higher than the correlations between interpersonal relations and the two products. These differences, however, were not significant at the .05 level. Concurring with the evidence by Epting [27, 28], these findings appear to provide some indication that the more similar the domains of interest the greater the likelihood that cognitive differentiation is generalizable across domains.[2]

Aberrations of the Fishbein Attitude Model: The Effects of Their Deletion on Study Results

The Fishbein attitude model states that a positive relationship exists between the predicted and elicited attitude. A number of researchers, however, have observed negative correlations between the elicited and predicted attitude measures for some respondents [e.g., 1, 89]. Ahtola [1], for example, found that approximately 50% of his respondents had correlations of 0 or less (negative correlations) when the Fishbein attitude model was employed and 34.7% when his matrix model was used.

A number of conceivable reasons exist why negative correlations may be encountered. One reason revolves around possible measurement errors in the instruments used to measure attitude, regardless of the specific model selected. A second reason, however, may be that for a segment of the population a linear compensatory attitude model, such as that proposed by Fishbein, is not satisfactory. Also, the respondent himself may be the causative factor due to fatigue, boredom, inability to understand

---

[2]The assumption made is that two product categories are more similar than comparing a product category to interpersonal relations.

what is being queried, or just perhaps a desire not to complete the questionnaire accurately.

In the preceding sections of this study, all respondents were included in the analysis regardless of whether negative correlations between the elicited and predicted measures of attitude were found to exist. The purpose of this section was to determine if the inclusion or exclusion of those respondents with negative correlations had any material effect on the acceptance or rejection of the research hypothesis. Hypotheses 1 and 2 were reanalyzed with the respondents who had negative correlations separated for analysis. The results of the reanalysis were compared to the earlier findings which included all respondents.

Hypothesis 1: Cognitive Differentiation and the Number of Cognitive Elements

Eliminating from the analysis those respondents who had negative correlation coefficients between predicted and elicited attitude produced no substantial change in the results for hypothesis 1. As shown in Tables 10 and 11, respondents with negative values seemed to do nothing more, except in the case of the peak determinism entrance procedure, than depress the hypothesized relationship for toothpaste.

There were, however, differences in the case of toothpaste between those respondents for which the model yielded negative and positive coefficients (negative and positive

TABLE 10

CORRELATIONS BETWEEN NUMBER OF COGNITIVE ELEMENTS AND COGNITIVE DIFFERENTIATION BY ENTRANCE METHOD FOR TOOTHPASTE AND AUTOMOBILES --ELEMENTS ENTERED IN THE SAME ORDER

	Peak Determinism	Significant Determinism	Peak Regression	Significant Regression	Peak Salience	Significant Salience
TOOTHPASTE						
Positive Values	-.130(85)	-.322(85)[a]	-.097(86)	-.024(88)	-.108(86)	-.053(83)
Negative Values	-.188(14)	.093(14)	-.363(13)	-.139(11)	.311(13)	-.083(16)
Total Sample[b]	-.161	-.138	-.057	-.310	-.040	-.074
AUTOMOBILES						
Positive Values	-.115(93)	-.015(91)	-.002(92)	-.014(93)	-.088(98)	-.065(96)
Negative Values	.065(9)	-.114(11)	-.246(10)	.000(9)	-.540(4)	-.345(6)
Total Sample[b]	-.030	-.026	-.106	-.076	-.024	-.021

[a] $p < .05$

[b] These coefficients are the same as those presented in Tables 4 and 5 when the analysis was based on the total sample.

TABLE 11

CORRELATIONS BETWEEN NUMBER OF COGNITIVE ELEMENTS AND COGNITIVE
DIFFERENTIATION BY ENTRANCE METHOD FOR TOOTHPASTE AND AUTOMOBILES
--ELEMENT ORDER ALLOWED TO VARY

	Peak Determinism	Significant Determinism	Peak Regression	Significant Regression
TOOTHPASTE				
Positive Values	-.175(83)	-.245(83)[a]	-.108(87)	-.059(87)
Negative Values	-.092(16)	-.046(16)	.056(12)	-.108(12)
Total Sample[b]	-.181	-.094	-.223	-.068
AUTOMOBILES				
Positive Values	-.051(93)	-.044(93)	-.018(94)	-.024(93)
Negative Values	.268(9)	.227(9)	-.332(8)	-.087(9)
Total Sample[b]	-.088	-.008	-.042	-.021

[a] $p < .05$

[b] These coefficients are the same as those presented in Tables 4 and 5 when the analysis was based on the total sample.

values). For the positive group, the optimal number of cognitive elements was significantly correlated with cognitive differentiation when the significant determinism entrance procedure was employed. No significant relationship was found for those respondents with negative correlation coefficients. Results remained unchanged for the other entrance procedures in the case of toothpaste.

The results for automobiles were not altered when those respondents with negatively correlated predicted and elicited attitude values were separated for analysis. In approximately half of the entrance procedures for automobiles, the inclusion of respondents with negative coefficients depressed the hypothesized correlation between cognitive differentiation and the number of cognitive elements. For the remaining entrance order procedures, the hypothesized correlation was higher, but not significantly, for those with negative correlation coefficients. The reason for the higher correlations is unclear. There is no theoretical basis for the hypothesized relationship between cognitive differentiation and the optimal number of cognitive elements to be stronger for those respondents with negative correlations than for those for whom the model produces positive correlations

Hypothesis 2: Predictive Efficacy of the Intra-Individual versus Cross-Sectional Analytical Procedures in the Attitude Model

Excluding those respondents who had negative correlations between the predicted and elicited attitude measures did not alter the conclusion that the intra-individual analytic procedure is more effective in predicting attitude than is the cross-sectional one. When those respondents for whom the attitude model produced negative correlations were eliminated from the analysis, the difference between the two approaches, cross-sectional versus intra-individual, was enlarged. This was due to the r to Z transformation in which the negative correlation coefficients were subtracted from the sum of the Z scores before the mean was computed. The subtraction had the effect of reducing the average Z score and therefore depressed the computed mean correlation between the elicited and predicted measures of attitude.

The mean correlation coefficients based on those respondents with negative and positive correlations are shown in Tables 12 through 15. The "total sample" coefficients correspond to those in Tables 6 and 7, and are, in fact, a weighted average for the positive and negative value coefficients for the sample as a whole. The mean correlation coefficients for the "positive values" were all significantly greater ($p<.05$) than the "total sample" coefficients when compared within each entrance procedure.

TABLE 12

MEAN CORRELATION COEFFICIENTS DERIVED FROM THE INTRA-INDIVIDUAL
ANALYSIS FOR TOOTHPASTE--COGNITIVE ELEMENTS
ENTERED IN THE SAME ORDER

	Peak Determinism	Significant Determinism	Peak Regression	Significant Regression	Peak Salience	Significant Salience
Positive Values	.852 (85)	.853 (85)	.869 (86)	.854 (88)	.846 (86)	.850 (83)
Negative Values	.662 (14)	.613 (14)	.592 (13)	.635 (11)	.656 (13)	.608 (16)
Total Sample	.750	.756	.788	.780	.751	.735

Note: The number of subjects used to complete the average correlation coefficients (via Fisher's r to z transformation) is in parentheses.

TABLE 13

MEAN CORRELATION COEFFICIENTS DERIVED FROM THE INTRA-INDIVIDUAL
ANALYSIS FOR TOOTHPASTE--COGNITIVE ELEMENT
ENTRANCE ORDER PERMITTED TO VARY

	Peak Determinism	Significant Determinism	Peak Regression	Significant Regression	Peak Salience	Significant Salience
Positive Values	.849(83)	.842(83)	.887(87)	.884(87)	.846(86)	.850(83)
Negative Values	.635(16)	.710(16)	.684(12)	.606(12)	.656(13)	.608(16)
Total Sample	.678	.709	.813	.814	.751	.735

Note: The number of subjects used to compute the average correlation coefficients (via Fisher's r to Z transformation) is in parentheses.

TABLE 14

MEAN CORRELATION COEFFICIENTS DERIVED FROM THE INTRA-INDIVIDUAL ANALYSIS FOR AUTOMOBILES--COGNITIVE ELEMENTS ENTERED IN THE SAME ORDER[a]

	Peak Determinism	Significant Determinism	Peak Regression	Significant Regression	Peak Salience	Significant Salience
Positive Values	.807(93)	.805(90)	.832(92)	.824(93)	.845(98)	.847(96)
Negative Values	678(9)	.681(12)	.725(10)	.749(9)	.803(4)	.678(6)
Total Sample	.738	.709	.756	.754	.817	.808

[a]The number of subjects used to compute the average correlation coefficients (via Fisher's r to Z transformation) is in parentheses.

TABLE 15

MEAN CORRELATION COEFFICIENTS DERIVED FROM THE INTRA-INDIVIDUAL ANALYSIS FOR AUTOMOBILES--COGNITIVE ELEMENT ENTRANCE ORDER PERMITTED TO VARY[a]

	Peak Determinism	Significant Determinism	Peak Regression	Significant Regression	Peak Salience	Significant Salience
Positive Values	.810(93)	.807(92)	.844(94)	.844(93)	.845(98)	.847(96)
Negative Values	.650(9)	.624(9)	.817(8)	.748(9)	.803(4)	.678(6)
Total Sample	.775	.738	.778	.778	.817	.808

[a]The number of subjects used to compute the average correlation coefficients (via Fisher's r to z transformation) is in parentheses.

This difference held regardless of whether or not the entrance order of the cognitive elements was permitted to vary.

A comparison of the positive value correlation coefficients for toothpaste (Tables 12 and 13) and automobiles (Tables 14 and 15) for their respective entrance procedure revealed no significant differences in the effectiveness of the attitude model for either product category in the intra-individual phase of the study. The same conclusion was reached in the previous discussion of hypothesis 2 when all respondents were included in the analysis. As stated earlier, one possible explanation for this is that the intra-individual analysis eliminates those biases due to combining heterogeneous response sets and anchor effects which occur in cross-sectional analysis. These results seem to indicate that the deletion of those respondents for whom the attitude model produces negative correlations may not substantially change the conclusions reached when all respondents are included in the analysis.

It should be noted, however, that the optimal number of cognitive elements and the degree of differentiation differed between the respondents in this study who had positive and negative correlations between predicted and elicited measures of attitude. Before concluding, therefore, that those respondents who deviate from the expected positive correlation should be combined in the analysis, one might wish to examine an additional set of findings

No discernable pattern exists between the mean differentiation scores between the two segments (positive and negative values) for automobiles (Tables 16 and 17). In some instances the mean differentiation score is greater for those respondents with negative values and in other instances the relationship is reversed.

Tables 18 and 19 show the differences in differentiation scores between those respondents with positive and negative values for toothpaste. The only instance in which the absolute mean differentiation score for negative values was less than the positive values was in the case of peak salience where the cognitive elements were entered in the same order (Table 19). In six of the remaining nine instances, the mean differentiation score for those respondents with positive values was significantly greater ($p<.05$) than for those with negative values.

Differences were found to exist between the two sets of respondents on the mean number of optimal elements. In the case of automobiles, the mean number of cognitive elements for those respondents with positive correlations (positive values) was significantly greater ($p<.05$) than the mean for those where the model yielded negative values. These differences existed both when the cognitive element

TABLE 16

MEAN COGNITIVE DIFFERENTIATION SCORES FOR AUTOMOBILES--COGNITIVE ELEMENT ENTRANCE ORDER PERMITTED TO VARY[a]

	Peak Determinism	Significant Determinism	Peak Regression	Significant Regression
Positive Value Differentiation	148.02(93)	146.70(93)	148.09(94)	148.38(93)
Negative Value Differentiation	149.78(9)	163.44(9)	149.25(8)	146.11(9)
Difference	1.76	16.74[b]	1.16	2.27

[a] The number of respondents from which the means were computed are in parentheses and may vary due to the influence of the entrance procedure on the correlation between the predicted and elicited attitudes.

[b] $p<.05$

TABLE 17

MEAN COGNITIVE DIFFERENTIATION SCORES FOR AUTOMOBILES--COGNITIVE ELEMENTS ENTERED IN SAME ORDER[a]

	Peak Determinism	Significant Determinism	Peak Regression	Significant Regression	Peak Salience	Significant Salience
Positive Value Differentiation	148.23(93)	147.59(91)	148.20(92)	147.96(93)	148.97(93)	149.26(96)
Negative Value Differentiation	147.67(9)	153.00(11)	148.00(10)	150.44(9)	128.75(4)	130.83(6)
Difference	0.56	5.41	0.20	2.48	20.22[b]	18.43[b]

[a]The number of respondents from which the means were computed are in parentheses and may vary due to the influence of the entrance procedure on the correlation between the predicted and elicited attitudes.

[b]$p<.05$

TABLE 18

MEAN COGNITIVE DIFFERENTIATION SCORES FOR TOOTHPASTE--COGNITIVE ELEMENT ENTRANCE ORDER PERMITTED TO VARY[a]

	Peak Determinism	Significant Determinism	Peak Regression	Significant Regression
Positive Value Differentiation	67.05(83)	67.30(83)	67.54(87)	67.46(87)
Negative Value Differentiation	71.88(16)	70.56(16)	69.92(12)	70.50(12)
Difference	4.83[b]	3.26[b]	2.38	3.04

[a]The number of respondents from which the means were computed are in parentheses and may vary due to the influence of the entrance procedure on the correlation between the predicted and elicited attitudes.

[b] $p < .05$

TABLE 19

MEAN COGNITIVE DIFFERENTIATION SCORES FOR TOOTHPASTE--COGNITIVE ELEMENTS ENTERED IN THE SAME ORDER[a]

	Peak Determinism	Significant Determinism	Peak Regression	Significant Regression	Peak Salience	Significant Salience
Positive Value Differentiation	66.93(85)	66.80(85)	67.45(86)	67.44(88)	68.29(86)	66.95(83)
Negative Value Differentiation	73.29(14)	74.07(14)	70.31(13)	70.91(11)	64.77(13)	72.38(16)
Difference	6.36[b]	7.27[b]	2.86	3.47[b]	3.52[b]	5.43[b]

[a]The number of respondents from which the means were computed are in parentheses and may vary due to the influence of the entrance procedure on the correlation between the predicted and elicited attitudes.

[b]$p < .05$

entrance order was not permitted to vary across respondents (Table 20) and when the entrance order was permitted to vary (Table 21).

It is interesting to note that the regression entrance procedures for automobiles produced a lower mean number of optimal cognitive elements than did any other entrance procedure. The entrance procedures which produced the fewest number of respondents with negative correlation coefficients were the salience approaches. In the peak and significant entrance procedures only approximately 4% and 6%, respectively, of the respondents had negative correlations compared to 8% to 10% for the significant and peak regression procedures presented in Tables 20 and 21.

For toothpaste (Tables 22 and 23), the mean number of cognitive elements for those with positive values was significantly greater (p<.05) than those with negative values in 3 out of 10 possible comparisons. In four of the other comparisons, the differences were significant at the .10 level. Insignificant differences between the means were found for peak regression when the elements were entered in the same order (Table 23) and for the significant and peak regression procedures where the element entrance order was permitted to vary (Table 22) In all comparisons the mean number of optimal cognitive elements for the positive values was larger in absolute terms than the negative values.

TABLE 20

MEAN NUMBER OF COGNITIVE ELEMENTS FOR AUTOMOBILES--COGNITIVE ELEMENT ENTRANCE ORDER PERMITTED TO VARY[a]

	Peak Determinism	Significant Determinism	Peak Regression	Significant Regression
Positive Values	6.96(93)	5.95(93)	4.47(94)	3.63(93)
Negative Values	2.33(9)	2.11(9)	1.88(8)	1.67(9)
Difference	4.63[b]	3.84[b]	2.59[b]	1.96[b]
Total Sample Mean	6.55	5.61	4.27	3.46

[a] The number of respondents from which the means were computed are in parentheses and may vary due to the influence of the entrance procedure on the correlation between the predicted and elicited attitudes.

[b] $p < .05$

TABLE 21

MEAN NUMBER OF COGNITIVE ELEMENTS FOR AUTOMOBILES--COGNITIVE ELEMENTS ENTERED IN SAME ORDER[a]

	Peak Determinism	Significant Determinism	Peak Regression	Significant Regression	Peak Salience	Significant Salience
Positive Values	7.18(93)	6.20(91)	5.49(92)	4.55(93)	6.64(98)	5.85(96)
Negative Values	2.00(9)	1.73(11)	1.30(10)	1.00(9)	3.25(4)	2.17(6)
Difference	5.18[b]	4.47[b]	4.19[b]	3.55[b]	3.39[b]	3.68[b]
Total Sample Mean	6.73	5.72	5.08	4.24	6.51	5.64

[a]The number of respondents from which the means were computed are in parentheses and may vary due to the influence of the entrance procedure on the correlation between the predicted and elicited attitudes.

[b]$p<.05$

TABLE 22

MEAN NUMBER OF COGNITIVE ELEMENTS FOR TOOTHPASTE--COGNITIVE
ELEMENTS ENTRANCE ORDER PERMITTED TO VARY[a]

	Peak Determinism	Significant Determinism	Peak Regression	Significant Regression
Positive Values	4.77(83)	4.01(83)	3.33(87)	2.86(87)
Negative Values	2.80(16)	2.63(16)	3.00(12)	2.42(12)
Difference	1.96[b]	1.38[b]	0.33	0.44
Total Sample Mean	4.46	3.79	3.29	2.81

[a]The number of respondents from which the means were computed are in parentheses and may vary due to the influence of the entrance procedure on the correlation between the predicted and elicited attitudes.

[b]$p<.05$

TABLE 23

MEAN NUMBER OF COGNITIVE ELEMENTS FOR DIFFERENT ENTRANCE PROCEDURES
AND COGNITIVE DIFFERENTIATION SCORE FOR TOOTHPASTE--COGNITIVE ELEMENTS ENTERED
IN THE SAME ORDER[a]

	Peak Determinism	Significant Determinism	Peak Regression	Significant Regression	Peak Salience	Significant Salience
Positive Values	4.69(85)	3.87(85)	3.67(86)	2.84(88)	4.26(86)	3.57(83)
Negative Values	2.71(14)	1.93(14)	3.23(13)	1.91(11)	2.92(13)	2.50(16)
Difference	1.98[b]	1.94[b]	0.44	0.93[c]	1.34[b]	1.07[c]
Total Sample Mean	4.41	3.59	3.62	2.74	4.08	3.39

[a]The number of respondents from which the means were computed are in parentheses and may vary due to the influence of the entrance procedure on the correlation between the predicted and elicited attitudes.

[b]$p<.05$

[c]$p<.10$

In comparing the entrance approaches as to the number of cognitive elements for toothpaste, the regression procedures again appeared to be more efficient in terms of having a lower mean number of cognitive elements entered into the attitude model. Fewer cognitive elements were found because the stepwise regression procedure takes into account the intercorrelation or similarity between the cognitive elements while entering the elements into the predictive equation. Furthermore, the significant entrance procedures, regardless of whether the element order was permitted to vary or remained stable, had fewer cognitive elements than their respective peak entrance procedure. These findings are the same as were found for automobiles. The only difference was that the salience procedures had approximately the same number of respondents with negative correlations between predicted and elicited attitude as did the other entrance procedures for toothpaste.

CHAPTER VI

CONCLUSION

Hypothesis 1: Cognitive Differentiation and the Number of Cognitive Elements

In examining the hypothesis that the optimal number of cognitive elements is positively related to cognitive differentiation, six different entrance procedures (e.g., significant determinism, peak regression) were used. They were applied in two ways: (1) the cognitive element order was permitted to vary and (2) all elements were entered in the same order across all respondents.

No significant correlation coefficients between the optimal number of cognitive elements and differentiation were found in the case of automobiles, although in all but one instance the relationships were in the predicted direction. Since the largest of the coefficients for toothpaste was .31 and accounted for only 9.5% of the variation, the null hypothesis was not rejected.

These results, although not significant, do indicate the possibility of a weak relationship between differentiation and the number of cognitive elements to be used in predicting attitude. Two possible reasons for the weak results may be the sample and the product categories employed in the study.

College students participated in this study. While the study was exploratory in nature, and no attempt was made to generalize the findings, the relatively homogeneous makeup of the sample may have reduced the possibility of significant results. This might have been due to the relative lack of variation in cognitive differentiation between respondents. A non-student sample should produce greater variation in differentiation scores.

The product categories selected were designed to fit at opposite ends of the complexity and involvement scale. Perhaps the results would have been significant if a third product category had been included that was less complex than automobiles but more complex than toothpaste. In other words, a product category in the middle range of complexity would have provided greater insight as to whether the hypothesized relationship is weak across all product categories rather than just the extreme ends of the continuum. A possibility of a "U" shape relationship is based on evidence that cognitive integration increases as the complexity of the environment increases up to some optimal level. Beyond that level integration begins to decrease [65]. It should be noted that a third product category was not included because of possible respondent fatigue and boredom which might have introduced noise into the results.

Hypothesis 2 Predictive Efficacy of the Intra-Individual versus Cross-Sectional Analytic Procedures in the Attitude Model

The results of this portion of the study indicate that the predictive efficiency of the attitude model is greater when the analytic procedure is based on an intra-individual analysis rather than a cross-sectional one An attempt to improve the predictive ability of the attitude model via cross-sectional analysis by standardizing the attitudinal components failed. In fact, a decrease in the correlation between the predicted and elicited measures of attitude resulted when the model was standardized This decrease was due to the redefinition of the cognitive element by the standardization process in a manner which is theoretically inconsistent with the Fishbein attitude model. The general conclusion, therefore, is that an intra-individual procedure should be used with the Fishbein attitude model if the predictive ability of the model is important. This conclusion is consistent with other studies [11, 56, 86].

One additional rationale behind using an intra-individual rather than cross-sectional analytic technique is the variation in the model's ability to predict attitude in different product categories. When a cross-sectional procedure was used there appeared to be substantial differences in the predictive ability of the model between autos and toothpaste. These differences disappeared, however, when the intra-individual approach was employed. Since there is no theoretical justification for these differences, they may be due either to the model's inappropriate representation of a specific individual's cognitive structure when viewed in a cross-sectional manner or because more heterogeneity existed in one product category than in another thereby causing differences in the model's predictive efficacy.

A major difficulty in utilizing results based on an intra-individual analytical framework for attitudinal research lies in the operationalization of the model and in the interpretation of the results. The problem revolves around which cognitive element entrance procedure should be employed in predicting attitudes and whether or not the entrance order of the cognitive elements should be permitted to vary between respondents. The secondary results of the analysis of this hypothesis pertain to these questions.

In the case of toothpaste, the salience entrance procedures (peak and regression) produced slightly higher correlations between predicted and elicited measures of attitude than any other procedure. On the other hand, the regression procedure was slightly better in the case of automobiles. A strong argument cannot be made for using one procedure over another, since the differences were slight and none of the entrance procedures had correlation coefficients below .73. The regression approach, however, is easier to implement than the others since no additional questions, such as importance of difference, need to be asked to order the elements for entry into the model. Furthermore, the regression procedure for both product categories appeared to be more parsimonious in terms of a lower mean number of optimal cognitive elements entered into the attitude model. The prediction of attitudes on the basis of fewer cognitive elements holds greater implications to the marketing manager in that it may be easier for the marketing practitioner to implement

No significant differences in the predictive efficacy of the attitude model were found between permitting the element order to vary across respondents and holding it constant across respondents. Since the interpretation of the data is facilitated greatly when the entrance order remains stable across respondents, this approach might be preferred by marketing practitioners.

Hypothesis 3: Generalizability of Cognitive Differentiation

Although the differentiation scores between toothpaste and automobiles were significantly correlated ($p<.05$), the null hypothesis was not rejected because the absolute sizes of the correlation coefficients were low. The coefficient was .3266 which is too low for the construct of differentiation to be considered generalizable in a managerial sense. If the product categories had been closer together in terms of either complexity of consumer interest, perhaps the correlations would have been higher. This would be consistent with previous findings that the more similar the domains of interest, the more likely that differentiation will be generalizable.

Areas for Further Research

Several major areas for future research became evident during the analysis of the findings. These areas include the use of a cognitive structural variable other than differentiation in examining hypothesis 1, a more in-depth examination of why the attitude model produces positive correlations for some respondents and negative ones for others, and the need for additional research on cognitive element entrance procedures.

Cognitive integration may be an appropriate structural variable of cognition in analyzing the hypothesis that the optimal number of cognitive elements are positively related to one's cognitive structure. Some of the findings between differentiation and the number of optimal elements included in the model (hypothesis 1) might have been insignificant because of how different individuals combine the cognitive elements in evaluating brands--cognitive integration. In other words, while two respondents with similar differentiation levels may have the same number of salient cognitive elements, one may be cognitively integrated where these elements are combined to produce new ones and one may not. The key may not be, therefore, how many cognitive elements are salient for a consumer but how they are integrated within his cognitive framework.

In this study, as in others, the correlation between the predicted and elicited measures of attitude was not positive for all respondents. One area for additional research is to attempt to determine the population for which the model does not yield positive correlations. Knowing this might help to correct what appears to be an aberration and thus perhaps obtain a more accurate understanding of attitudes.

In the case of cognitive element entrance procedures, additional research needs to be performed. While the present study introduced the concept of a "significant" entrance procedure, no staged entrance procedure appeared to dominate in terms of the predictive efficacy of the attitude model. As other researchers have noted [e.g., 56, 88], additional research is necessary into determining a staged entrance procedure which closely approximates an individual's analysis of product information. Through the use of a more appropriate entrance procedure perhaps hypothesis 1 would have been supported. A final area for future research revolves around attempting to ascertain whether a strong relationship exists between easily identified market segments and cognitive differentiation and integration. Cognitive differentiation and/or integration may be useful in attempting to explain why some consumers process more information than others and why different attitudes are formed toward the same object.

APPENDICES

APPENDIX I-A

TOOTHPASTE INSTRUMENT

FORM A

TOOTHPASTE

In this section of the questionnaire we are interested in your judgments concerning several brands of <u>toothpaste</u> as well as certain characteristics of them. When filling out the questionnaire, please make your judgments on the basis of what these things mean <u>to you</u>. Since we are interested only in your own personal view, there are <u>no right or wrong answers</u>.

This is how you are to use the scales in judging the brands and characteristics of toothpaste:

If you feel that the concept at the top of the page is very closely related to one end of the scale, you should place your check-mark as follows:

good X : ___ : ___ : ___ : ___ : ___ : ___ bad

or

good ___ : ___ : ___ : ___ : ___ : ___ : X   bad

If you feel that the concept is quite closely related to one or the other end of the scale (but not extremely), you should place your check-mark as follows:

strong ___ : X : ___ : ___ : ___ : ___ : ___ weak

or

strong ___ : ___ : ___ : ___ : ___ : X : ___ weak

If the concept seems only slightly related to one side as opposed to the other side (but is not really neutral), then you should check as follows:

new ___ : ___ : _X_ : ___ : ___ : ___ : ___ old

or

new ___ : ___ : ___ : ___ : _X_ : ___ : ___ old

The direction toward which you check, of course, depends upon which of the two ends of the scale seem most characteristic of the item you are judging. If you consider the concept to be <u>neutral</u> on the scale, both sides of the scale <u>equally associated</u> with the concept, or if the scale is <u>completely irrelevant</u>, unrelated to the concept, then you should place your check-mark in the middle space:

good ___ : ___ : ___ : _X_ : ___ : ___ : ___ bad

<u>IMPORTANT</u>: (1) Place your check-marks <u>in the middle of spaces</u>, not on the boundaries:

    THIS   NOT THIS
___ : ___ : _X_ : ___ : _X_ ___ : ___

(2) Be sure you check every scale for every concept--<u>do not omit any</u>.

(3) Never put more than one check-mark on a single scale.

Sometimes you may feel as though you've answered the same item before. This will not be the case, so please <u>do not look back and forth</u> through the items. Do not try to remember how you checked similar items earlier. <u>Make each item a separate and independent judgment</u>. Work at a fairly high speed throughout. Do not worry or puzzle over individual items. It is your first impressions, your immediate feelings about the items, that we want. On the other hand, please do not be careless, because we want your true impressions.

A toothpaste which is white in color is:

good ___ : ___ . ___ . ___ : ___ : ___ : ___ bad

A toothpaste which is expensive is:

good ___ : ___ : ___ : ___ : ___ : ___ : ___ bad

A toothpaste which has a pleasant taste/flavor is:

good ___ ___ . ___ : ___ : ___ : ___ bad

A toothpaste which is high on cavity prevention ingredients is:

good ___ . ___ : ___ : ___ : ___ : ___ bad

A toothpaste which has a smooth texture is:

good ___ . ___ . ___ . ___ : ___ . ___ : ___ bad

A toothpaste which is high on whitening/brightening ingredients is:

good ___ : ___ : ___ . ___ . ___ : ___ : ___ bad

A toothpaste which is high on ingredients for cleaning teeth is:

good ___ : ___ : ___ : ___ : ___ : ___ bad

A toothpaste which is high on breath freshening ingredients is:

good ___ . ___ : ___ : ___ : ___ : ___ . ___ bad

The next series of questions asks you to make judgments as to the probability that a particular characteristic or attribute is related to a brand of toothpaste. Please judge each brand along each characteristic whether you are familiar with the brands or not. Again, there are no correct or incorrect answers.

What is the probability that each of the following toothpaste brands has a smooth texture?

Close-up   :probable ___:___:___:___:___:___ improbable
Pepsodent   :probable ___:___:___:___:___:___ improbable
Pearl Drops :probable ___:___:___:___:___:___ improbable
McClean's   :probable ___:___:___:___:___:___ improbable
Colgate   :probable ___:___:___:___:___:___ improbable
Gleem II   :probable ___:___:___:___:___:___ improbable
Ultra Brite :probable ___:___:___:___:___:___ improbable
Crest   :probable ___:___:___:___:___:___ improbable

What is the probability that each of the following toothpaste brands is high on cavity prevention ingredients?

Pepsodent   :probable ___:___:___:___:___:___ improbable
Colgate   :probable ___:___:___:___:___:___ improbable
Ultra Brite :probable ___:___:___:___:___:___ improbable
Gleem II   :probable ___:___:___:___:___:___ improbable
Pearl Drops :probable ___:___:___:___:___:___ improbable
Crest   :probable ___:___:___:___:___:___ improbable
Close-up   :probable ___:___:___:___:___:___ improbable
McClean's   :probable ___:___:___:___:___:___ improbable

What is the probability that each of the following brands is high on breath freshening ingredients?

Crest   :probable ___:___:___:___:___:___:___ improbable
Gleem II   :probable ___:___:___:___:___:___:___ improbable
Colgate   :probable ___:___:___:___:___:___:___ improbable
Pearl Drops   :probable ___:___:___:___:___:___:___ improbable
Close-up   :probable ___:___:___:___:___:___:___ improbable
Ultra Brite   :probable ___:___:___:___:___:___:___ improbable
Pepsodent   :probable ___:___:___:___:___:___:___ improbable
McClean's   :probable ___:___:___:___:___:___:___ improbable

What is the probability that each of the following toothpaste brands is high on whitening/brightening ingredients?

McClean's   :probable ___:___:___:___:___:___:___ improbable
Colgate   :probable ___:___:___:___:___:___:___ improbable
Pepsodent   :probable ___:___:___:___:___:___:___ improbable
Pearl Drops   :probable ___:___:___:___:___:___:___ improbable
Gleem II   :probable ___:___:___:___:___:___:___ improbable
Close-up   :probable ___:___:___:___:___:___:___ improbable
Crest   :probable ___:___:___:___:___:___:___ improbable
Ultra Brite   :probable ___:___:___:___:___:___:___ improbable

What is the probability that each of the following toothpaste brands is expensive?

Close-up   :probable ___:___:___:___:___:___:___ improbable
McClean's   :probable ___:___:___:___:___:___:___ improbable
Crest   :probable ___:___:___:___:___:___:___ improbable
Pepsodent   :probable ___:___:___:___:___:___:___ improbable
Pearl Drops   :probable ___:___:___:___:___:___:___ improbable

Colgate   :probable ___:___:___:___:___:___:___ improbable

Ultra Brite:probable ___:___:___:___:___:___ ___ improbable

Gleem II   .probable ___:___:___.___:___:___ improbable

What is the <u>probability</u> that each of the following toothpaste brands is <u>high on ingredients for cleaning teeth</u>?

Gleem II   :probable ___:___:___:___:___:___ improbable

Colgate   :probable ___:___:___:___:___:___ improbable

Crest   :probable ___:___:___:___:___:___ improbable

Ultra Brite:probable ___:___:___:___:___:___ improbable

McClean's   :probable ___:___:___:___:___:___ improbable

Pearl Drops:probable ___:___:___:___:___:___ improbable

Pepsodent   .probable ___:___:___:___:___:___ improbable

Close-up   :probable ___:___:___:___:___:___ improbable

What is the <u>probability</u> that each of the following toothpaste brands has a <u>pleasant taste/flavor</u>?

Pearl Drops:probable ___:___:___:___:___:___ improbable

Crest   probable ___:___.___:___:___:___ improbable

Close-up   :probable ___:___:___:___:___:___ improbable

McClean's   ·probable ___:___.___:___:___:___ improbable

Pepsodent   :probable ___ ___:___:___.___:___ improbable

Ultra Brite:probable ___.___.___:___:___:___ improbable

Gleem II   probable ___ ___.___·___·___:___ improbable

Colgate   ·probable ___·___:___:___:___:___ improbable

What is the probability that each of the following toothpaste brands is white in color?

Colgate	:probable	___:___:___:___:___:___:___	improbable
Ultra Brite	:probable	___:___:___:___:___:___:___	improbable
Pearl Drops	:probable	___:___:___:___:___:___:___	improbable
Close-up	:probable	___:___:___:___:___:___:___	improbable
Crest	:probable	___:___:___:___:___:___:___	improbable
McClean's	:probable	___:___:___:___:___:___:___	improbable
Gleem II	:probable	___:___:___:___:___:___:___	improbable
Pepsodent	:probable	___:___:___:___:___:___:___	improbable

Please rate each of the following brands of toothpaste relative to its appeal to you. Place an X under the category which most closely corresponds to your feelings.

	Extremely High Appeal	High Appeal	Mildly High Appeal	Neutral	Mildly Low Appeal	Low Appeal	Extremely Low Appeal
Crest has :	___ :	___ :	___ :	___ :	___ :	___ :	___
Pearl Drops has :	___ :	___ :	___ :	___ :	___ :	___ :	___
McClean's has :	___ :	___ :	___ :	___ :	___ :	___ :	___
Close-up has :	___ :	___ :	___ :	___ :	___ :	___ :	___
Gleem II has :	___ :	___ :	___ :	___ :	___ :	___ :	___
Colgate has :	___ :	___ :	___ :	___ :	___ :	___ :	___

	Extremely High Appeal	High Appeal	Mildly High Appeal	Neutral	Low Appeal	Mildly Low Appeal	Extremely Low Appeal
Ultra Brite has :	___ :	___ .	___ :	___ :	___ :	___ :	___
Pepsodent has :	___ :	___ .	___ :	___	___ :	___ :	___

Please rate the following attributes as to their <u>importance</u> to you in selecting a brand of toothpaste. Place an X under the category which most closely corresponds to your feelings.

	Extremely Important	Very Important	Moderately Important	Slightly Important	No Importance
breath freshening ability	___ :	___ .	___ .	___ :	___
smooth texture	___ :	___ .	___	___ :	___
expensive	___ :	___ :	___ :	___ :	___
white in color	___ :	___	___	___ :	___
pleasant taste/ flavor	___ :	___ :	___ :	___ :	___
ability to clean teeth	___ .	___	___ .	___ :	___
whitening/ brightening ability	___ :	___	___ .	___ :	___
ability to prevent cavities	___ :	___ :	___ .	___ :	___

Please rate how much difference you feel there is among toothpaste brands (McClean's, Close-up, Gleem II, Pearl Drops, Crest, Colgate, Ultra Brite, Pepsodent) along each of the following attributes. Please an X under the category which more closely corresponds to your feelings.

	Extreme Differences	Large Differences	Moderate Differences	Slight Differences	No Differences
color	___:	___:	___:	___:	___
texture (smooth-gritty)	___:	___:	___:	___:	___
price	___:	___:	___:	___:	___
breath freshening ability	___:	___:	___:	___:	___
taste/flavor	___:	___:	___:	___:	___
whitening/brightening ability	___:	___:	___:	___:	___
ability to clean teeth	___:	___:	___:	___:	___
ability to prevent cavities	___:	___:	___:	___:	___

Toothpaste Grid Instructions

This section of the questionnaire is designed to help understand the way people think about different brands of toothpaste. Since we are interested in your own opinions, there are no right or wrong answers

On the next page a grid is provided which contains a number of brands of toothpaste and a series of characteristics or attributes associated with each brand. Lay the grid sideways so that the short side of the page is up and down and the long side runs left and right. The brands should now be at the top of the page and the attributes on the right side of the page

Please rate each of the eight brands of toothpaste along each of the attributes. For example, the first attribute is pleasant taste/flavor--unpleasant taste/flavor. The six numbers along the top of the words refer to the six points along this scale. A +3 indicates that a brand has a very pleasant taste/flavor, a +2 indicates a pleasant taste/flavor, and +1 indicates a slightly pleasant taste/flavor, a -1 indicates a slightly unpleasant taste/flavor, a -2 indicates an unpleasant taste/flavor, and a -3 a very unpleasant taste/flavor

After you have given a rating to each of the brands for the pleasant-unpleasant taste/flavor attribute, go on to the next row. Please finish one row before going on to the next and do not leave any squares blank.

132

	+3	+2	+1	-1	-2	-3
	PLEASANT TASTE/FLAVOR			UNPLEASANT TASTE/FLAVOR		
	EXPENSIVE			INEXPENSIVE		
	WHITE			COLORED		
	SMOOTH TEXTURE			GRITTY TEXTURE		
	FRESHENS BREATH			DOES NOT FRESHEN BREATH		
	CLEANS TEETH			DOES NOT CLEAN TEETH		
	PREVENTS CAVITIES			DOES NOT PREVENT CAVITIES		
	WHITENS/BRIGHTENS			DOES NOT WHITEN/BRIGHTEN		
	+3	+2	+1	-1	-2	-3

RATING GRID

	Pearl Drops	Colgate	Pepsodent	Gleem II	Close-up	Crest	Ultra Brite	McClean's
Row 1								
Row 2								
Row 3								
Row 4								
Row 5								
Row 6								
Row 7								
Row 8								

APPENDIX I-B

AUTOMOBILES INSTRUMENT

FORM B

AUTOMOBILES

In this section of the questionnaire we are interested in your judgments concerning several brands of <u>automobiles</u> as well as certain characteristics of them. When filling out the questionnaire, please make your judgments on the basis of what these things mean <u>to you</u>. Since we are interested only in your own personal views, there are <u>no right or wrong answers</u>.

This is how you are to use the scales in judging the brands and characteristics of automobiles:

If you feel that the concept at the top of the page is very closely related to one end of the scale, you should place your check-mark as follows:

good <u>X</u> : ___ : ___ : ___ : ___ : ___ : ___ bad

or

good ___ : ___ : ___ : ___ : ___ : ___ : <u>X</u> bad

If you feel that the concept is quite closely related to one or the other end of the scale (but not extremely), you should place your check-mark as follows:

strong ___ : <u>X</u> : ___ : ___ : ___ : ___ : ___ weak

or

strong ___ : ___ : ___ : ___ : ___ : <u>X</u> : ___ weak

If the concept seems only slightly related to one side as opposed to the other side (but is not really neutral), then you should check as follows:

new ___ : ___ : _X_ : ___ : ___ : ___ old

or

new ___ : ___ : ___ : _X_ : ___ : ___ old

The direction toward which you check, of course, depends upon which of the two ends of the scale seem most characteristic of the item you are judging. If you consider the concept to be <u>neutral</u> on the scale, both sides of the scale <u>equally associated</u> with the concept, or if the scale is <u>completely irrelevant</u>, unrelated to the concept, then you should place your check-mark in the middle space:

good ___ : ___ : ___ : _X_ : ___ : ___ : ___ bad

IMPORTANT: (1) Place your check-marks <u>in the middle of spaces</u>, not on the boundaries:

      THIS   NOT THIS

___ : ___ : _X_ : ___ : _X_ ___ : ___

(2) Be sure you check every scale for every concept--<u>do not omit any</u>.

(3) Never put more than one check-mark on a single scale

Sometimes you may feel as though you've answered the same item before. This will not be the case, so please <u>do not look back and forth</u> through the items. Do not try to remember how you checked similar items earlier. <u>Make each item a separate and independent judgment</u>. Work at a fairly high speed throughout Do not worry or puzzle over individual items. It is your first impressions, your immediate feelings about the items, that we want. On the other hand, please do not be careless, because we want your true impressions.

An automobile which is economical is:

good ___ : ___ : ___ : ___ : ___ : ___ : ___ bad

A high performance automobile is.

good ___ : ___ : ___ : ___ : ___ : ___ : ___ bad

A luxurious automobile is:

good ___ : ___ : ___ : ___ : ___ : ___ : ___ bad

A highly dependable automobile is:

good ___ : ___ : ___ : ___ : ___ : ___ : ___ bad

An automobile which handles poorly is:

good ___ : ___ : ___ : ___ : ___ : ___ : ___ bad

An automobile which gets poor gas mileage is:

good ___ : ___ : ___ : ___ : ___ : ___ : ___ bad

An automobile which is of high quality is:

good ___ : ___ : ___ : ___ : ___ : ___ : ___ bad

An automobile which is comfortable is:

good ___ : ___ : ___ : ___ : ___ : ___ : ___ bad

An automobile which has unattractive styling is.

good ___ : ___ : ___ : ___ : ___ : ___ : ___ bad

An automobile which is large is:

good ___ : ___ : ___ : ___ : ___ : ___ : ___ bad

The next series of questions asks you to make judgments as to the probability that a particular characteristic or attribute is related to an automobile model and make. Please judge each automobile along each characteristic whether you are familiar with the brands or not. Again, there are no correct or incorrect answers.

What is the probability that each of the following automobiles is small?

Maverick
(Ford)   :probable ___:___:___:___:___:___ improbable

Nova
(Chevrolet) :probable ___:___:___:___:___:___ improbable

Road Runner
(Plymouth) :probable ___:___:___:___:___:___ improbable

Dart (Dodge):probable ___:___:___:___:___:___ improbable

Mustang II
(Ford)   :probable ___:___:___:___:___:___ improbable

Cutlass
(Oldsmobile):probable ___:___:___:___:___:___ improbable

Vega (Chevro-
let)   :probable ___:___:___:___:___:___ improbable

Pinto (Ford):probable ___:___:___:___:___:___ improbable

Javelin (Ameri-
can Motors) :probable ___:___:___:___:___:___ improbable

Beetle (VW) :probable ___:___:___:___:___:___ improbable

What is the probability that each of the following automobiles is luxurious?

Road Runner
(Plymouth) :probable ___:___:___:___:___:___ improbable

Maverick
(Ford)   probable ___:___:___:___:___:___ improbable

Pinto (Ford):probable ___:___:___:___:___:___ improbable

Nova
(Chevrolet) :probable ___:___:___:___:___:___ improbable

Vega
(Chevrolet) :probable ___:___:___:___:___ ___ improbable

Javelin (AMC):probable ___:___:___:___:___·___ improbable

Cutlass
(Oldsmobile):probable ___:___:___:___:___:___ improbable

Beetle (VW)   probable ___:___:___:___:___:___ improbable

Dart (Dodge):probable ___:___:___·___·___:___ improbable

Mustang II
(Ford)   :probable ___:___:___:___:___:___ improbable

What is the <u>probability</u> that each of the following automobiles <u>handles poorly</u>?

Vega
(Chevrolet) :probable ___:___:___:___:___·___ improbable

Nova
(Chevrolet) :probable ___:___·___:___:___:___ improbable

Cutlass
(Oldsmobile):probable ___ ___:___·___:___·___:___ improbable

Javelin (AMC):probable ___:___:___:___:___·___ improbable

Maverick
(Ford)   :probable ___:___:___:___:___ ___ improbable

Beetle (VW) :probable ___·___:___:___ ___·___ improbable

Mustang II
(Ford)   :probable ___:___:___:___ ___:___ improbable

Dart (Dodge).probable ___·___:___:___·___·___ improbable

Pinto (Ford):probable ___:___:___:___ ___:___ improbable

Road Runner
(Plymouth) :probable ___:___·___:___·___:___ improbable

What is the <u>probability</u> that each of the following is a <u>high performance</u> automobile?

Dart (Dodge)·probable ___:___:___ ___ ___:___ improbable

Nova
(Chevrolet) :probable ___:___:___·___·___:___ improbable

Mustang II
(Ford)   :probable ___:___:___:___:___ ___:___ improbable

Cutlass
(Oldsmobile):probable ___.___:___:___:___:___ improbable

Maverick
(Ford)   :probable ___:___:___:___:___:___ improbable

Javelin (AMC):probable ___:___:___:___ ___.___ improbable

Pinto (Ford):probable ___:___:___:___:___:___ improbable

Beetle (VW) :probable ___.___:___:___:___.___ improbable

Vega
(Chevrolet) :probable ___:___:___:___:___.___ improbable

Road Runner
(Plymouth)   :probable ___:___:___:___:___:___ improbable

What is the <u>probability</u> that each of the following automobiles is <u>highly dependable</u>?

Javelin (AMC):probable ___:___:___:___:___:___ improbable

Road Runner
(Plymouth)   .probable ___:___:___:___:___:___ improbable

Pinto (Ford)·probable ___:___:___:___:___:___ improbable

Dart (Dodge) probable ___:___:___:___:___:___ improbable

Vega
(Chevrolet) :probable ___:___ ___:___:___:___ improbable

Cutlass
(Oldsmobile):probable ___:___:___:___:___:___ improbable

Beetle (VW) :probable ___.___ ___ ___:___:___ improbable

Maverick
(Ford)   :probable ___:___:___.___:___:___ improbable

Mustang II
(Ford)   :probable ___.___:___:___.___:___ improbable

Nova
(Chevrolet) :probable ___:___ ___:___.___.___ improbable

What is the <u>probability</u> that each of the following automobiles is <u>comfortable</u>?

Beetle (VW) .probable ___:___:___:___.___:___:___ improbable

Mustang II
(Ford) :probable ___:___:___ ___.___:___:___ improbable

Nova
(Chevrolet) :probable ___:___:___:___ ___:___:___ improbable

Pinto (Ford):probable ___:___:___:___:___:___:___ improbable

Cutlass
(Oldsmobile) ·probable ___.___:___:___:___:___ improbable

Dart (Dodge):probable ___:___:___:___:___:___ improbable

Maverick
(Ford) :probable ___:___:___:___ ___.___·___ improbable

Javelin (AMC).probable ___:___:___:___:___:___:___ improbable

Road Runner
(Plymouth) :probable ___ ___:___:___:___·___·___ improbable

Vega
(Chevrolet) :probable ___·___:___:___.___:___:___ improvable

What is the <u>probability</u> that each of the following automobiles gets <u>poor gas mileage</u>?

Mustang II
(Ford) :probable ___:___ ___:___:___:___ ___ improbable

Dart (Dodge):probable ___:___·___:___:___:___:___ improbable

Beetle (VW) :probable ___ ___:___:___:___:___ ___ improbable

Road Runner
(Plymouth) :probable ___:___.___ ___:___:___:___ improbable

Nova
(Chevrolet) :probable ___ ___:___:___:___:___:___ improbable

Vega
(Chevrolet) ·probable ___:___ ___.___:___:___:___ improbable

Javelin (AMC):probable ___:___:___:___·___:___:___ improbable

Cutlass
(Oldsmobile):probable ___:___:___:___:___:___:___ improbable

Pinto (Ford) probable ___:___:___:___:___:___:___ improbable

Maverick
(Ford)   :probable ___:___:___:___:___:___:___ improbable

What is the <u>probability</u> that each of the following automobiles is <u>economical</u>?

Cutlass
(Oldsmobile):probable ___ ___:___:___:___:___:___ improbable

Vega
(Chevrolet) probable ___ ___:___:___:___:___:___ improbable

Nova
(Chevrolet) .probable ___:___:___:___:___:___:___ improbable

Beetle (VW) :probable ___:___:___:___:___:___:___ improbable

Dart (Dodge).probable ___:___:___:___:___:___:___ improbable

Road Runner
(Plymouth) :probable ___:___:___:___:___:___:___ improbable

Mustang II
(Ford)   :probable ___:___:___ ___:___:___:___ improbable

Pinto (Ford).probable ___:___:___:___:___:___:___ improbable

Maverick
(Ford)   :probable ___:___:___:___:___:___ ___ improbable

Javelin (AMC):probable ___:___:___ ___ ___:___:___ improbable

What is the <u>probability</u> that each of the following automobiles is of <u>high quality</u>?

Javelin (AMC):probable ___:___:___:___:___:___:___ improbable

Maverick
(Ford)   :probable ___:___:___:___:___:___:___ improbable

Dart (Dodge):probable ___:___:___ ___:___:___:___ improbable

Mustang II
(Ford)   .probable ___:___:___:___:___:___:___ improbable

Beetle (VW) :probable ___:___:___:___:___:___:___ improbable

Vega
(Chevrolet) .probable ___:___:___:___:___:___ ___ improbable

Pinto (Ford): probable ___:___:___:___:___:___:___ improbable

Road Runner
(Plymouth) : probable ___:___:___:___:___:___:___ improbable

Nova
(Chevrolet) : probable ___:___:___:___:___:___:___ improbable

Cutlass
(Oldsmobile): probable ___:___:___:___:___:___:___ improbable

What is the <u>probability</u> that each of the following automobiles has <u>attractive styling</u>?

Cutlass
(Oldsmobile): probable ___:___:___:___:___:___:___ improbable

Road Runner
(Plymouth) : probable ___:___:___:___:___:___:___ improbable

Javelin AMC) : probable ___:___:___:___:___:___:___ improbable

Pinto (Ford): probable ___:___:___:___:___:___:___ improbable

Nova
(Chevrolet) : probable ___:___:___:___:___:___:___ improbable

Dart (Dodge): probable ___:___:___:___:___:___:___ improbable

Vega
(Chevrolet) : probable ___:___:___:___:___:___:___ improbable

Maverick
(Ford) : probable ___:___:___:___:___:___:___ improbable

Beetle (VW) : probable ___:___:___:___:___:___:___ improbable

Mustang II
(Ford) : probable ___:___:___:___:___:___:___ improbable

Please rate each of the following automobiles relative to its <u>appeal</u> to you. Place an X under the category which most closely corresponds to your feelings

	Extremely High Appeal	High Appeal	Mildly High Appeal	Neutral	Low Appeal	Mildly Low Appeal	Extremely Low Appeal
Beetle (VW) has :	___	___	___	___	___	___	___
Cutlass (Olds) has :	___	___	___	___	___	___	___
Pinto (Ford) has :	___	___	___	___	___	___	___
Road Runner (Ply.) has :	___	___	___	___	___	___	___
Javelin (AMC) has :	___	___	___	___	___	___	___
Maverick (Ford) has :	___	___	___	___	___	___	___
Dart (Dodge) has :	___	___	___	___	___	___	___
Nova (Chev.) has :	___	___	___	___	___	___	___
Vega (Chev) has :	___	___	___	___	___	___	___
Mustang II (Ford) has :	___	___	___	___	___	___	___

Please rate the following attributes as to their <u>importance</u> to you in selecting an automobile. Place an X under the category which most closely corresponds to your feelings.

	Extremely Important	Very Important	Moderately Important	Slightly Important	No Importance
attractive styling	: ___ :	___ :	___ :	___ :	___
high performance	: ___ :	___ :	___ :	___ :	___
dependability	: ___ :	___ :	___ :	___ :	___
gas mileage	: ___ :	___ :	___ :	___ :	___
handling	: ___ :	___ :	___ :	___ :	___
comfort	: ___ :	___ :	___ :	___ :	___
luxury	: ___ :	___ :	___ :	___ :	___
economy	: ___ :	___ :	___ :	___ :	___
quality	: ___ :	___ :	___ :	___ :	___
size	: ___ :	___ :	___ :	___ :	___

Please rate how much <u>difference</u> you feel there is among automobiles (Javelin, Road Runner, Pinto, Dart, Vega, Cutlass, Beetle, Maverick, Mustang II, Nova) along each of the following attributes. Place an X under the category which more closely corresponds to your feelings.

	Extreme Differences	Large Differences	Moderate Differences	Slight Differences	No Differences
gas mileage	: ___ :	___ :	___ :	___ :	___
size	: ___ :	___ :	___ :	___ :	___
quality	: ___ :	___ :	___ :	___ :	___
economy	: ___ :	___ :	___ :	___ :	___

	Extreme Differ- ences	Large Differ- ences	Moderate Differ- ences	Slight Differ- ences	No Differ- ences
styling	: ___ :	___ :	___ :	___ .	___
dependability	: ___ :	___ :	___ .	___ :	___
comfort	: ___ :	___ .	___ :	___ .	___
handling	: ___ :	___ :	___ :	___ .	___
luxury	: ___ :	___ :	___ :	___	___
performance	: ___	___ :	___ :	___ .	___

Automobile Grid Instructions

This section of the questionnaire is designed to help understand the way people think about different automobiles. Since we are interested in your own opinions there are no right or wrong answers.

On the next page a grid is provided which contains a number of different automobiles and a series of characteristics or attributes associated with each one. Lay the grid sideways so that the short side of the page is up and down and the long side runs left and right. The automobiles should now be at the top of the page and the attributes on the right side of the page.

Please rate each of the 10 automobiles along each of the attributes. For example, the first attribute is good gas mileage-poor gas mileage. The six numbers along the top of the wrods refer to the six points along this scale. A +3 indicates that the automobile gets very good gas mileage, a +2 indicates that an automobile gets good gas mileage, a +1 indicates that the automobile gets slightly good gas mileage, a -1 indicates a slightly poor gas mileage, a -2 indicates a poor gas mileage, and a -3 indicates a very poor gas mileage.

After you have given a rating to each of the brands for the gas mileage attribute, go on to the next row. Please finish one row before going on to the next and do not leave any squares blank.

RATING GRID

	+3 +2 +1	-1 -2 -3		Beetle (VW)	Cutlass (Olds)	Pinto (Ford)	Road Runner (Ply.)	Javelin (AMC)	Maverick (Ford)	Dart (Dodge)	Nova (Chev.)	Vega (Chev.)	Mustang II (Ford)
Row 1	GOOD GAS MILEAGE	POOR GAS MILEAGE											
Row 2	HIGH QUALITY	LOW QUALITY											
Row 3	HIGH PERFORMANCE	LOW PERFORMANCE											
Row 4	LARGE	SMALL											
Row 5	DEPENDABLE	UNDEPENDABLE											
Row 6	ECONOMICAL	UNECONOMICAL											
Row 7	ATTRACTIVE STYLING	UNATTRACTIVE STYLING											
Row 8	COMFORTABLE	UNCOMFORTABLE											
Row 9	LUXURIOUS	NOT LUXURIOUS											
Row 10	GOOD HANDLING	POOR HANDLING											
	+3 +2 +1	-1 -2 -3											

APPENDIX I-C

INTERPERSONAL GRID INSTRUMENT

Interpersonal Grid Instructions

This section of the questionnaire is designed to help understand the way people think about different people. Since we are interested in your own opinions there are no right or wrong answers.

On the next page a grid is provided which contains a number of "role persons" (e.g., mother, father, yourself) and a series of characteristics or attributes associated with each one. Lay the grid sideways so that the short side of the page is up and down and the long side runs left and right. The "role persons" should now be at the top of the page and the characteristics on the right side of the page.

Beginning with your own name, write the first names of the person described in the space to the right of that person. If you cannot remember a person's name, write something about him (her) which will clearly bring to your mind the person's identity. DO NOT USE ANY NAME MORE THAN ONCE.

After you have written each person's name, please rate each of the 10 individuals along each characteristic. For example, the first characteristic is outgoing-shy. The six numbers along the top of the words refer to the six points along this scale. A +3 indicates very outgoing; a +2 indicates moderately outgoing; a +1 indicates slightly outgoing; a -1 indicates <u>slightly</u> shy; a -2 indicates <u>moderately</u> shy; and a -3 indicates <u>very</u> shy.

Once you have given a rating to each person for the outgoing-shy characteristic, go on to the next row. <u>Please finish one row before going on to the next and do not leave any squares blank.</u>

RATING GRID

	+3 +2 +1	-1 -2 -3
	OUTGOING	SHY
	ADJUSTED	MALADJUSTED
	DECISIVE	INDECISIVE
	CALM	EXCITABLE
	INTERESTED IN OTHERS	SELF ABSORBED
	CHEERFUL	ILL HUMORED
	RESPONSIBLE	IRRESPONSIBLE
	CONSIDERATE	INCONSIDERATE
	INDEPENDENT	DEPENDENT
	INTERESTING	DULL
	+3 +2 +1	-1 -2 -3

Brief Description of Columns	Row 1	Row 2	Row 3	Row 4	Row 5	Row 6	Row 7	Row 8	Row 9	Row 10
1. Yourself										
2. Person you dislike										
3. Mother										
4. Person you'd like to help										
5. Father										
6. Friend of same sex										
7. Friend of opposite sex										
8. Person you feel uncomfortable with										
9. Instructor										
10. Person difficult to understand										

APPENDIX I-D

QUESTIONNAIRE
(Toothpaste)

Please describe the following brands of toothpaste with respect to the following characteristics (cavity prevention, cleaning teeth, texture, freshen breath, price, taste/flavor, whiten/brighten, and color).

Give a description of the brand only in terms of the characteristic of the toothpaste and not in terms of any evaluative judgment of the toothpaste brand; i.e., not in terms of your preference or dislike of the toothpaste.

Give each description independently and not in comparison with any other brands.

Thank you for your cooperation.

	Close-up	McClean's	Crest	Gleem II	Pearl Drops	Ultra Brite	Pepsodent	Colgate
Cavity Prevention								
Cleaning Teeth								
Texture								
Freshen Breath								
Price								
Taste/flavor								
Whiten/brighten								
Color								

APPENDIX I-E

QUESTIONNAIRE
(Automobiles)

Please describe the following brands of automobiles with respect to the following characteristics (comfort, gas mileage, size, handling, economy, luxury, performance, quality, dependability, and styling.

Give a description of the brand not only in terms of the characteristics of the automobile and *not* in terms of any evaluative judgment of the automobile; i.e., not in terms of your preference or dislike of the automobile.

Give each description independently and not in comparison with any other brands.

Thank you for your cooperation.

	Javelin (American Motors)	Cutlass (Oldsmobile)	Beetle (VW)	Dart (Dodge)	Mustang II (Ford)	Road Runner (Plymouth)	Maverick (Ford)	Pinto (Ford)	Nova (Chevrolet)	Vega (Chevrolet)
Comfort										
Gas Mileage										
Size										
Handling										
Economy										
Luxury										
Performance										
Quality										
Dependability										
Styling										

APPENDIX II

FREQUENCY DISTRIBUTION OF CORRELATION COEFFICIENTS

II-A

FREQUENCY DISTRIBUTION OF CORRELATION COEFFICIENTS FOR TOOTHPASTE WITH VARIABLES ENTERED ON INTRA-INDIVIDUAL BASIS (n = 99)

Entrance Procedure

r Interval	Peak Determinism	Significant Determinism	Peak Regression	Significant Regression
.91 to 1.0	24	23	33	33
.81 to .9	23	24	22	20
.71 to .8	11	9	13	13
.61 to .7	9	9	10	8
.51 to .6	5	5	1	4
.41 to .5	5	4	2	3
.31 to .4	6	4	4	3
.21 to .3		5	2	3
.11 to .2				
.01 to 1				
0 to -.1				
-.11 to -.2				
-.21 to -.3			1	1
-.31 to -.4	4	2	1	2
-.41 to -.5	1	2	1	1
-.51 to -.6				
-.61 to -.7	5	5	6	5
-.71 to -.8	2	3	2	2
-.81 to -.9	2	2	1	1
-.91 to -1.0	2	2		

II-B

FREQUENCY DISTRIBUTION OF CORRELATION COEFFICIENTS FOR TOOTHPASTE WITH VARIABLES ENTERED IN SAME ORDER (n = 99)

r Interval	Peak Determinism	Significant Determinism	Peak Regression	Significant Regression	Peak Salience	Significant Salience
.91 to 1.0	25	24	33	32	25	22
.81 to .9	20	22	16	15	23	25
.71 to .8	17	15	9	10	10	10
.61 to .7	5	6	11	11	9	9
.51 to .6	8	7	8	7	6	6
.41 to .5	3	4	5	4	2	2
.31 to .4	6	6	4	6	11	6
.21 to .3	1	1	1	2		3
.11 to .2				1		
.01 to .1						
0 to -.1						
-.11 to -.2						
-.21 to -.3			1			
-.31 to -.4	2	2	3	1	3	6
-.41 to -.5	2	3	1	3	1	1
-.51 to -.6	1	3	2	1	1	2
-.61 to -.7	5	3	3	4	5	4
-.71 to -.8	2	2			1	1
-.81 to -.9	1		2	2	1	1
-.91 to -1.0	1	1			1	1

II-C

FREQUENCY DISTRIBUTION OF CORRELATION COEFFICIENTS
FOR AUTOMOBILES WITH VARIABLES ENTERED IN
SAME ORDER (n = 102)

Entrance Procedure

r Interval	Peak Determinism	Significant Determinism	Peak Regression	Significant Regression	Peak Salience	Significant Salience
.91 to 1.0	12	13	13	22	21	20
.81 to .9	29	27	25	24	41	38
.71 to .8	25	24	26	26	23	27
.61 to .7	15	12	8	6	6	6
.51 to .6	7	9	4	7		
.41 to .5	4	3	4	4	3	2
.31 to .4		1	1	2	2	2
.21 to .3	1		2	2	2	1
.11 to .2		1				
.01 to .1						
0 to -.1						
-.11 to -.2						1
-.21 to -.3						
-.31 to -.4	2	2	1	1		1
-.41 to -.5	1	1	1			
-.51 to -.6	2	3	2	2		
-.61 to -.7	2	3	2	2	2	2
-.71 to -.8					1	1
-.81 to -.9	1	2	3	3		
-.91 to -1.0	1	1	1	1	1	1

II-D

FREQUENCY DISTRIBUTION OF CORRELATION COEFFICIENTS FOR AUTOMOBILES WITH VARIABLES ENTERED ON INTRA-INDIVIDUAL BASIS (n = 102)

Entrance Procedure

r Interval	Peak Determinism	Significant Determinism	Peak Regression	Significant Regression
.91 to 1.0	15	14	19	19
.81 to .9	26	27	32	32
.71 to .8	26	25	22	21
.61 to .7	14	13	9	10
.51 to .6	7	8	4	4
.41 to .5	3	2	4	4
.31 to .4	1	2	3	3
.21 to .3	1	1		
.11 to .2		1		
.01 to 0.1				
0 to -.1				
-.11 to -.2				
-.21 to -.3	1	1		
-.31 to -.4	3	2	3	3
-.41 to -.5				
-.51 to -.6	1	1		
-.61 to -.7	2	3	2	2
-.71 to -.8			2	2
-.81 to -.9	1	1	1	1
-.91 to -1.0	1	1	1	1

REFERENCES

1. Ahtola, Olli T. *An Investigation of Cognitive Structure Within Expectancy x Value Response Models.* Doctoral dissertation, The University of Illinois, 1972.

2. Ajzen, Icek and Martin Fishbein. "Attitudinal and Normative Variables as Predictors of Specific Behaviors: A Review of Research Generated by a Theoretical Model," paper presented at the Workshop on Attitude Research and Consumer Behavior, University of Illinois, 1970.

3. Allard, Marvel and Earl R. Carlson. "The Generality of Cognitive Complexity," *Journal of Social Psychology*, 59 (February 1963), 73-5.

4. Allport, G. W. "The Historical Background of Modern Social Psychology," in G. Lindzey, ed., *Handbook of Social Psychology*, Vol. 1 Cambridge, Massachusetts: Addison-Wesley, 1954, 3-56.

5. Alpert, Mark I. "Identification of Determinant Attributes: A Comparison of Methods," *Journal of Marketing Research*, 8 (May 1971), 184-91.

6. Attneave, Fred. *Applications of Information Theory to Psychology.* New York. Holt-Dryden, 1959.

7. Bannister, D. and J. M. M. Mair. *The Evaluation of Personal Constructs.* New York: Academic Press, 1968.

8. Bass, Frank M. "Fishbein and Brand Preferences: A Reply," *Journal of Marketing Research*, 9 (November 1972), 461.

9. Bass, Frank M., Edgar A. Pessemier, and Donald R. Lehmann. "An Experimental Study of Relationships Between Attitudes, Brand Preference and Choice," Institute Paper No. 307, Krannert Graduate School of Industrial Administration, Purdue University, 1971.

10. Bass, Frank M. and W. Wyne Talarzyk. "An Attitude Model for the Study of Brand Preference," *Journal of Marketing Research*, 9 (February 1972), 93-6.

11. Bass, Frank M. and William L. Wilkie. "A Comparative Analysis of Attitudinal Predictions of Brand Preference," *Journal of Marketing Research*, 10 (August 1973), 262-9.

12. Bieri, James. "Cognitive Complexity and Judgment of Inconsistent Information," in Robert P. Abelson et al., eds., *Theories of Cognitive Consistency: A Sourcebook*. U.S.A.: Rand McNally & Co., 1968, 633-40.

13. Bieri, James. "Cognitive Complexity and Personality Development," in O. J. Harvey, ed., *Experience, Structure and Adaptability*. New York: Springer Publishing Company, 1966, 13-37.

14. Bieri, James. "Cognitive Complexity: Assessment Issues in the Study of Cognitive Structure," paper presented as part of a symposium on "The Cognitive Approach to Personality Assessment," American Psychological Association, 1965.

15. Bieri, James. "Cognitive Structures in Personality," in Harold M. Schroder and Peter Suedfeld, eds., *Personality Theory and Information Processing*. U.S.A.: Ronald Press Company, 1971, 178-208.

16. Bieri, James. "Complexity-Simplicity as a Personality Variable in Cognitive and Preferential Behavior," in Donald W. Fiske and Salvatore R. Maddi, eds., *Functions of Varied Experience*. Homewood, Illinois: The Dorsey Press, Inc., 1961, 355-79.

17. Bieri, James, Alvin L. Alkines, and Scott Briar et al. *Clinical and Social Judgment: The Discrimination of Behavioral Information*. New York: John Wiley & Sons, Inc., 1966, 182-206.

18. Bither, Stewart and Stephen J. Miller. "A Cognitive Theory View of Brand Preference," *Proceedings*. Fall Conference, American Marketing Association, 1969, 280-6.

19. Bonarius, J. C. J. "Research in the Personal Construct Theory of George A. Kelly: Role Construct Repertory Test and Basic Theory," in Brendan A. Maher, ed., Progress in Experimental Personality Research, Vol. 2. New York: Academic Press, 1965, 2-46.

20. Chapman, W. S. "Some Observations on 'A User's Guide to Fishbein,'" Journal of the Market Research Society, 12 (July 1970), 166-8.

21. Churchill, Gilbert A. "Linear Attitude Models: A Study of Predictive Ability," Journal of Marketing Research, 9 (November 1972), 423-6.

22. Cohen, Joel B. and Olli T. Ahtola. "An Expectancy x Value Analysis of the Relationship Between Consumer Attitudes and Behavior," Proceedings. Second Annual Conference Association for Consumer Research, 1971, 344-64.

23. Cohen, Joel B., Martin Fishbein, and Olli T. Ahtola. "The Nature and Uses of Expectancy-Value Models in Consumer Attitude Research," Journal of Marketing Research, 9 (November 1972), 456-60.

24. Crockett, Walter H. "Cognitive Complexity and Impression Formation," in Brendan A. Maher, ed., Progress in Experimental Personality Research, Vol. 2. New York: Academic Press, 1965, 47-90.

25. Dixon, W. J., ed. Biomedical Computer Programs, 3rd edition. Los Angeles: University of California Press, 1973.

26. Draper, N. R. and H. Smith. Applied Regression Analysis. New York: John Wiley & Sons, Inc., 1966.

27. Epting, Franz R. Cognitive Complexity and Persuasibility Across Domains. Doctoral dissertation, Ohio State University, 1967.

28. Epting, Franz R. "The Stability of Cognitive Complexity in Construing Social Issues," British Journal of Social and Clinical Psychology, 11 (June 1972), 122-5.

29. Fishbein, Martin. "A Behavior Theory Approach to the Relations Between Beliefs About an Object and the Attitude Toward the Object," in Martin Fishbein, ed., Readings in Attitude Theory and Measurement. New York: John Wiley & Sons, Inc., 1967, 389-400.

30. Fishbein, Martin. "A Consideration of Beliefs and Their Roles in Attitude Measurement," in Martin Fishbein, ed., Readings in Attitude Theory and Measurement. New York: John Wiley & Sons, Inc., 1967, 257-66.

31. Fishbein, Martin. "A Consideration of Beliefs, Attitudes, and Their Relationship," in Ivan D. Steiner and Martin Fishbein, eds., Current Studies in Social Psychology. New York: Holt, Rinehart and Winston, Inc., 1965, 107-120.

32. Fishbein, Martin. "Attitude and the Prediction of Behavior," in Martin Fishbein, ed., Readings in Attitude Theory and Measurement. New York: John Wiley & Sons, Inc., 1967, 477-92.

33. Fishbein, Martin and Icek Ajzen. "Attitudes and Opinion," in Paul H. Mussen and Mark R. Rosenzweig, eds., Annual Review of Psychology, Vol. 23. Palo Alto, California: Annual Reviews, Inc., 1972, 188-544.

34. Guilford, J. P. Fundamental Statistics in Psychology and Education. New York: McGraw-Hill Book Company, 1964.

35. Hansen, Flemming. "Consumer Choice Behavior: An Experimental Approach," Journal of Marketing Research, 6 (November 1969), 436-43.

36. Harvey, O. J., David E. Hunt, and Harold M. Schroder. Conceptual Systems and Personality Organization. New York: John Wiley & Sons, Inc., 1961.

37. Hull, C. L. Principles of Behavior. New York: Appleton-Century, 1943.

38. Irwin, Marc, Tony Tripodi, and James Bieri. "Affective Stimulus Value and Cognitive Complexity," *Journal of Personality and Social Psychology*, 5 (April 1967), 444-8.

39. Jaspers, J. M. F. "Individual Cognitive Structures," paper presented to the Seventeenth International Congress of Psychology, 1963.

40. Kaplan, K. J. and Martin Fishbein. "The Source of Beliefs, Their Saliency and Prediction of Attitude," *Journal of Social Psychology*, 78 (June 1969), 63-74.

41. Katz, Daniel and Ezra Stotland. "A Preliminary Statement to a Theory of Attitude Structure and Change," in Sigmund Koch, ed., *Psychology: A Study of Science*, Vol. 3. New York: McGraw-Hill Book Company, Inc., 1959, 423-75.

42. Kelly, George A. *A Theory of Personality: The Psychology of Personal Constructs*. New York: W. W. Norton & Co., Inc., 1955.

43. Kelly, George A. "Europe's Matrix of Decision," in M. R. Jones, ed., *Nebraska Symposium on Motivation*. Lincoln: University of Nebraska Press, 1962.

44. Kelly, George A. *The Psychology of Personal Constructs*. New York: W. W. Norton & Co., Inc., 1955, 2 Vols.

45. Kelly, J. V. "A Programme for Processing George Kelly's Rep Grids on the IBM 1620 Computer," unpublished paper, Ohio State University, 1963.

46. King, Charles W. and John O. Summers. "Overlap of Opinion Leadership Across Consumer Product Categories," *Journal of Marketing Research*, 7 (February 1970), 43-50.

47. Klippel, R. Eugene. *An Experimental Evaluation of Attitude Change as a Relevant Factor in the Allocation of Advertising Funds: A Cognitive Approach*. Doctoral dissertation, The Pennsylvania State University, 1971.

48. Klippel, R. Eugene and Stewart W. Bither. "Attitude Data in Allocation Models," *Journal of Advertising Research*, 12 (April 1972), 20-4.

49. Kothandapani, Virupaksha. "Validation of Feeling, Belief, and Intention To Act as Three Components of Attitude and Their Contribution to Prediction of Contraceptive Behavior," *Journal of Personality and Social Psychology*, 19 (September 1971), 321-33.

50. Krech, David, Richard S. Crutchfield, and Egerton L. Ballachey. *Individual in Society*. New York: McGraw-Hill Book Company, Inc., 1962.

51. Mazis, Michael B. and R. Eugene Klippel. "A Comparison of Four Expectancy-Value Formulations in the Prediction of Consumer Attitudes," *Proceedings*. Fourth Annual Conference, Association for Consumer Research, 1973.

52. Miller, George A. "The Magical Number Seven, Plus or Minus Two: Some Limits on our Capacity for Processing Information," *Psychological Review*, 63 (March 1956), 81-97.

53. Miller, Henry and James Bieri. "Cognitive Complexity as a Function of the Significance of the Stimulus Objects Being Judges," *Psychological Reports*, 16 (June 1965), 1203-4.

54. Moinpour, Reza and Douglas L. MacLachlan. "The Relations Among Attribute and Importance Components of the Rosenberg-Fishbein Type Attitude Models: An Empirical Investigation," *Proceedings*. Second Annual Conference, Association for Consumer Research, 1971, 365-75.

55. Myers, James H. and Mark I. Alpert. "Determinant Buying Attitudes: Meaning and Measurement," *Journal of Marketing*, 32 (October 1968), 13-20.

56. Nakanishi, Masao and James R. Bettman. "Attitude Models Revisited: An Individual Level Analysis," *Journal of Consumer Research*, 1 (December 1974), 16-21).

57. Peak, Helen. "Attitude and Motivation," in Marshal R. Jones, ed., <u>Nebraska Symposium on Motivation</u>. Lincoln: University of Nebraska Press, 1955, 149-89.

58. Rigney, Joan, James Bieri, and Tony Tripodi. "Social Concept Attainment and Cognitive Complexity," <u>Psychological Reports</u>, 15 (October 1964), 503-9.

59. Rokeach, Milton. <u>Beliefs, Attitudes, and Values</u>. California: Jossey-Bass, Inc., 1968.

60. Rosenberg, Milton J. "A Structural Theory of Attitude Dynamics," <u>Public Opinion Quarterly</u>, 24 (Summer 1960), 319-40.

61. Rosenberg, Milton J. "Cognitive Structure and Attitudinal Affect," <u>Journal of Abnormal and Social Psychology</u>, 53 (November 1956), 367-72.

62. Rosenberg, Milton J. "Inconsistency, Arousal and Reduction in Attitude Change," in Ivan D. Steiner and Martin Fishbein, eds., <u>Current Studies in Social Psychology</u>. New York: Holt, Rinehart & Winston, Inc., 1965, 121-34.

63. Rosenberg, Milton J. and Carl I. Hovland. "Cognitive, Affective and Behavioral Components of Attitude," in Milton J. Rosenberg et al., eds., <u>Attitude Organization and Change</u>. New Haven, Connecticut: Yale University Press, Inc., 1960, 1-14.

64. Sampson, Peter and Paul Harris. "A User's Guide to Fishbein," <u>Journal of the Market Research Society</u>, 12 (July 1970), 145-66.

65. Schroder, Harold M., Michael J. Driver, and Siegfried Streufert. <u>Human Information Processing</u>. New York: Holt, Rinehart & Winston, 1967.

66. Schroder, Harold M. and Siegfried Streufert. "The Measurement of Four Systems of Personality Structure Varying in Level of Abstractness: Sentence Completion Method," Princeton University: ONR Technical Report No. 11, 1962.

67. Scott, Jerome E. and Peter B. Bennett. "Cognitive Models of Attitude Structure: Value Importance Is Important," *Proceedings*. Fall Conference of the American Marketing Association, 1971, 346-50.

68. Scott, William A. "Attitude Measurement," in Gardner Lindsay and Elliot Aronson, eds., *Handbook of Social Psychology*, Vol. 2, second edition. Reading, Massachusetts. Addison-Wesley Publishing Co., 1968, 204-73.

69. Scott, William A. "Brief Report: Measures of Cognitive Structure," *Multivariate Behavioral Research*, 12 (July 1966), 261-78.

70. Scott, William A. "Cognitive Complexity and Cognitive Balance," *Sociometry*, 26 (March 1963), 66-74.

71. Scott, William A. "Cognitive Complexity and Cognitive Flexibility," *Sociometry*, 25 (December 1962), 405-414.

72. Scott, William A. "Structural Properties of Cognition: Research Plan and Progress Report," unpublished paper, University of Colorado, 1972.

73. Scott, William A. "Structure of Natural Cognition," *Journal of Personality and Social Psychology*, 12 (August 1969), 261-78.

74. Shaw, Marvin E. and Jack M. Wright. *Scales for the Measurement of Attitudes*. New York: McGraw-Hill Book Company, 1967.

75. Sheth, Jagdish N. "Reply to Comments on the Nature and Uses of Expectancy-Value Models in Consumer Attitude Research," *Journal of Marketing Research*, 9 (November 1972), 462-5.

76. Sheth, Jagdish N. and W. Wayne Talarzyk. "Perceived Instrumentality and Value Importance as Determinants of Attitudes," *Journal of Marketing Research*, 9 (February 1972), 6-9.

77. Snedecor, George W. *Statistical Methods*. Ames, Iowa: Iowa State University Press, 5th edition, 1956, 173-7.

78. Streufert, Siegfried and Howard L. Fromkin. "Cognitive Complexity and Social Influence," in James T. Tedeschi, ed., *The Social Influence Processes*. Chicago, Illinois: Aldine-Atherton, Inc., 1972, 150-96.

79. Streufert, Susan C. "Cognitive Complexity: A Review," Purdue University: ONR Technical Report No. 2, 1972.

80. Swanson, Richard M. "Research in Developing Measures of Cognitive Differentiation," unpublished paper, University of Colorado, 1966.

81. Thurstone, L. L. "The Measurement of Social Attitudes," in Martin Fishbein, ed., *Readings in Attitude Theory and Measurement*. New York: John Wiley & Sons, Inc., 1967, 42-50.

82. Tripodi, Tony and James Bieri. "Cognitive Complexity as a Function of Own and Provided Constructs," *Psychological Reports*, 13 (August 1963), 26.

83. Tripodi, Tony and James Bieri. "Cognitive Complexity Perceived Conflict, and Certainty," *Journal of Personality*, 34 (March 1966), 144-53.

84. Tripodi, Tony and James Bieri. "Information Transmission in Clinical Judgments as a Function of Stimulus Dimensionality and Cognitive Complexity," *Journal of Personality*, 32 (March 1964), 119-37.

85. Vannoy, Joseph S. "Generality of Cognitive Complexity-Simplicity as a Personality Construct," *Journal of Personality and Social Psychology*, 2 (March 1965), 385-96.

86. Wilkie, William L. and John M. McCann. "The Halo Effect and Related Issues in Multi-Attribute Attitude Models--An Experiment," Institute Paper No. 377, Krannert Graduate School of Industrial Administration, Purdue University, 1972.

87. Wilkie, William L. and Edgar A. Pessemier. "Issues in Marketing's Use of Multi-Attribute Attitude Models," *Journal of Marketing Research*, 10 (November 1973), 428-41.

88. Wilkie, William L. and Rolf P. Weinreich. "Effects of the Number and Type of Attributes Included in an Attitude Model: More Is Not Better," Proceedings. Third Annual Conference, Association for Consumer Research, 1972, 325-40.

89. Witkin, H. A., D. R. B. Dyke, and H. F. Faterson et al. Psychological Differentiation. New York: John Wiley & Sons, 1962.

90. Woodworth, R. S. and H. Schlosberg. Experimental Psychology. New York: Holt, Rinehart & Co., 1954.

91. Wyer, Robert S. "Assessment and Correlates of Cognitive Differentiation and Integration," Journal of Personality, 32 (September 1964), 495-509.

92. Zajonc, Robert B. "Cognitive Theories in Social Psychology," in Gardner Lindsay and Elliot Aronson, eds., Handbook of Social Psychology, Vol. 1, second edition. Reading, Massachusetts: Addison-Wesley Publishing Co., 1968, 320-411.

93. Zajonc, Robert B. "The Process of Cognitive Tuning in Communication," Journal of Abnormal and Social Psychology, 61 (Summer 1960), 159-67.

Additional References

Bass, Frank M. and William L. Wilkie. "Perceived Instrumentality and Value Importance as Determinants of Attitudes," Journal of Marketing Research, 9 (February 1972), 93-6.

Bither, Stewart and Alan H. Shuart. "On Applying Expectancy-Value Attitude Models in Marketing Research," Working Series in Marketing Research, College of Business Administration, The Pennsylvania State University, No. 14, 1972.

Fishbein, Martin and Ronda Hunter. "Summation Versus Balance in Attitude Organization and Change," Journal of Abnormal and Social Psychology, 69 (November 1964), 505-10.

Fishbein, Martin and Bertram H. Raven. "The AB Scales: An Operational Definition of Belief and Attitude," in Martin Fishbein, ed., *Readings in Attitude Theory and Measurement*. New York: John Wiley & Sons, Inc., 1967, 183-9.

French, Vera V. "The Structure of Sentiments. I. A Restatement of the Theory of Sentiments," *Journal of Personality*, 15 (June 1957), 247-82.

French, Vera V. "The Structure of Sentiments. II. A Preliminary Study of Sentiments," *Journal of Personality*, 16 (September 1947), 78-108.

Lehmann, Donald R. Television Show Preference: Application of Choice Model," *Journal of Marketing Research*, 8 (February 1971), 47-55.

Lewin, Kurt. *Field Theory in Social Science*. New York: Harper, 1951.

Lutz, Richard J. "Investigating the Feasibility of Personalized Rapid Transit: An Experimental Approach," *Proceedings*. Third Annual Conference, Association for Consumer Research, 1972, 800-6.

McGuire, William J. "The Nature of Attitudes and Attitude Change," in Gardner Lindsay and Elliot Aronson, ed., *The Handbook of Social Psychology*, Vol. 3, second edition. Reading, Massachusetts: Addison-Wesley Publishing Co., 1968, 136-314.

Osgood, Charles E., George J. Suci, and Percy H. Tannenbaum. *The Measurement of Meaning*. Urbana. University of Illinois Press, 1957.

Scott, William A. "A Model and Measures of Cognitive Structure, unpublished paper, University of Colorado, 1966.

Scott, William A. "Conceptualizing and Measuring Structural Properties of Cognition," in O. J. Harvey, ed., *Motivation and Social Interaction: Cognitive Determinants*. New York: Ronald Press Company, 1963, 266-88.

Scott, William A. "The Structure of Natural Cognitions," unpublished paper, University of Colorado, 1967.

Scott, William A. "Values and Cognitive Systems," paper presented to the Annual Meeting of the American Psychological Association, 1972.

Smith, M. Brewster, Jerome S. Bruner, and Robert W. White. *Opinions and Personality*. New York: John Wiley & Sons, Inc., 1956.

BIOGRAPHICAL SKETCH

Richard M. Durand was born on November 7, 1947, in New York City. He received his primary education in New Jersey and later Cuba, where he lived for five years.

After returning from Cuba, he settled in Miami and graduated from Coral Gables Senior High School. In the fall of 1965, he entered the University of Florida and in 1968 received a B.A. degree in political science. He immediately began studying for his master's in business administration choosing marketing as his major field. After receiving his M.B.A. in 1970, he proceeded to enter the Ph.D. program in business administration at the University of Florida. The Ph.D. was conferred in August 1975.

Richard M. Durand is presently an Assistant Professor of Marketing at Southern Illinois University in Carbondale. He is married to Ileene Sehrt and they have one child, Richard Vernon.

CPSIA information can be obtained at www.ICGtesting.com
Printed in the USA
LVOW11s0011031013

355125LV00017BA/657/P